# BREAKING
# THE GLASS
# CEILING

# BREAKING THE GLASS CEILING

^ ˅

# WITHOUT BREAKING YOURSELF

## SUMMERS BOUTWELL

Clovercroft Publishing

Breaking the Glass Ceiling Without Breaking Yourself

© 2019 by Summers Boutwell

Published by Clovercroft Publishing, Franklin, Tennessee

Edited by Christy Callahan

Cover Design by Nelly Sanchez

Photograph by Monica Reyes

Interior Design by Adept Content Solutions

Printed in the United States of America

ISBN     978-1-948484-74-9

You're imperfect, and you're wired for struggle,
but you are worthy of love and belonging.
—Brené Brown

This book is dedicated to my mother, Laura Dunaway.
She has been a faithful, daily support in countless ways.
I admire that her life is a beautiful
illustration of someone who lives out her calling
and purpose to impact those around her.

# Contents

ʌ ⌄

# Acknowledgments

The completion of this book is a great example of living out one's purpose. It was a calling that resulted from a culmination of many experiences, challenges, and joys. Over the last year, I wrestled and dug deep with this topic to gain clarity of how I can best support you, the reader, to live a transformational life and not an exhausting one.

I'm so appreciative of this journey and had tremendous support from many family and friends. I'm thankful for Tammy Kling and Tiara Tompkins, from On Fire Books, for guiding me along the way. And I could not have done it without my husband (Sean Boutwell), my mother (Laura Dunaway), my father (Philip Dunaway), and many others, (Eric Dunaway, Kelly Christian, Joye Jones) who provided much support to help make this book a reality. I am grateful for your love and encouragement.

# The Manifesto of the Modern Woman

1. Living your purpose is transformational.
2. Being transparent is liberating, and it connects you to others.
3. Finding lasting balance comes from focusing on your relationships.
4. Being honest about what you want in this life and acting on it will bring you joy.
5. Being aware of what you need to improve is how you rise to the next level.
6. Learning to embrace imperfection will give you more energy and balance.
7. Listening and acting on your quiet inner voice will guide you toward your purpose. The more you act on it, the louder and clearer it will become.
8. Asking for help and helping others brings you balance and genuine relationships.

# INTRODUCTION

## The Phenomenon of the Modern Woman

Have you thought that with the next promotion, or, if you're an entrepreneur, with the next big achievement, you would be satisfied with your job? Or perhaps you've wondered if you completed a checklist of things in your life, things would be perfect?

Humans tend to be performance driven. Maybe that's how God wired us to be, naturally progressing in a way of always doing more and being more, or perhaps it's just a function we perform in autopilot. I think both are true. God has placed goals and dreams in our hearts, yet a lot of what we do is unintentional or on autopilot, and we believe that we need to do it to be happy. But when you do achieve these dreams, why isn't it quite as fulfilling as you had thought it would be?

Look, achievements are great. We all need goals and dreams. But there can come a point where you fall into the trap of chasing everyone else's dreams and success models with the result that you become overworked, overscheduled, and overstressed. It is so easy to fall into this trap because you are exerting much energy but never moving forward—juggling work, family, and all that comes with life. And in the end you lose focus on your key purposes in life.

If you have an undeviating focus on the finish line, you can face destruction and collateral damage in the journey to get there. In the process, the satisfaction and joy can be stripped away. This is where you may find the risk of breaking your relationships in the pursuit for success. The pressures that we humans face drive us to focus on the finish line, but because we have so much pressure on us, we don't have the time or energy to focus on the journey.

What if you could focus on the journey instead?

Once you learn those secrets of success, you can share them. You can provide a path for women to be more comfortable talking about and dealing with the struggles of modern life and help them find solutions to it. You can give hope to others to provide a better path to joy. You can redefine success and your perception of success to be focused on relationships and selflessness versus attaining more things, more status, and more power. Personally, I don't want people to let circumstances and expectations of the world blind them to the joy in the moment and joy in the journey. I want to challenge you to allow yourself to embrace those moments and to choose those moments that are most important to you.

Who is the modern woman? She is tough in the boardroom, nurturing with her family, and thoughtful with her friends, all the while taking care of herself physically to be healthy and strong. The modern woman is brave and confident—at all times. She is full of energy in juggling and leading in all the roles of her life—as a partner, mother, employee, leader, friend, sister, and daughter. The modern woman is expected to do the impossible of finding the perfect balance and providing the most impact in all of her spheres of influence.

Have you struggled with meeting the standards of the modern woman? I am this modern woman, and I have a confession: I am tired and exhausted. I admit that I cannot meet the standards that have been set forth for the modern woman. I am tired of the pressures (some of which are self-inflicted from competitiveness and guilt) to be the perfect wife, the best mom, a great friend, to take care of myself, and at the same time have a successful career. Trying to do it all—and trying to do it a—perfectly. In this quest for perfection, of course, I have found that it is not attainable, and I am constantly feeling like a failure in many areas of my life. I am tired of this volatility and tired of failing to give to what matters the most to me in this life—the relationships I treasure.

Have you felt the same forces in your own life? You are not alone.

The revelation of how far off the definition of the modern woman has become has overwhelmed my soul and catapulted me to break open the conversation on this topic. Why is it that many women are scared to talk about how difficult it is to be the modern woman? Is it because of the perception that it could derail women's efforts to drive equality or that it depicts a weakness? How often do you let society determine your feelings of your own success measured against a standard that is impossible to meet?

As I look around, I see broken women, broken families, and broken relationships. As I intentionally talked to women about this topic, there emerged a theme that women and families are under unbearable pressure and silently bearing the journey alone. I was amazed at the common themes that I heard from these women, of not being able to juggle career, family, or relationships successfully and how tired and alone the modern woman finds herself. When will we come to the humbling realization that we cannot do it all (even though we keep trying)?

Sometimes when you keep things to yourself in a dark corner, they fester and grow into bigger, unsurmountable pressures, becoming veritable monsters of self-doubt. If left unchecked—something you are left to figure out on your own—they can wreak havoc on your sense of self-worth. It almost seems taboo to talk about these things. Yet when I allowed myself to be transparent and opened up to other women that I was struggling in this area, I was taken aback with relief—from the both of us! When I was honest about how I felt, they completely related to the same challenges. The floodgates opened up for them to share and hear that it wasn't only they themselves who were suffering in this manner and that they were not alone. The weight of so much pressure on each woman was so apparent, and I saw how our current culture has stifled this all-pervasive issue.

This should no longer be kept in a dark corner. You should not be meeting this challenge feeling alone! As Tavi Gevinson said, "Sometimes if you expose your vulnerability, someone else will feel comforted. It's like we're all in this boat together."

We have made much headway with women's equality, but this superficial, unrealistic culture of generic success that has consumed us is very lonely, unfulfilling, and self-destructive. While we now have an equal opportunity to be leaders in the workplace, none of our other roles have diminished or disappeared. Not only do we have more opportunity, but we have added more complexity to our lives with families living farther apart and extra support from families becoming less of an option. We have become so busy that we don't have time to form deep bonds or nurture those deep relationships. As we divide our time and energy, inevitably something gets squeezed out. And ultimately, it falls to you to make the hard sacrifices. How do you choose one top priority over another? It's a recipe for madness.

Has the drive toward equality adversely affected the success of our family, the deepening of our friendships? With this deterioration of relationships in our culture, coupled with the unattainable pressures, we have set up a path for failure for the modern woman.

The role of the modern woman is truly amazing. But you know what, the endless pursuit of success, balance, and purpose is exhausting. And with that it is so easy to hide behind your busyness as an excuse not to pursue your true calling and purpose. So how do you break the glass ceiling without breaking yourself or your family in the process? How do we lead a life of intentional purpose that is transformational not exhausting?

Personally, my faith is a pillar in my life. My relationship with God guides me to pursue a higher calling. I have found that such purpose should be and is transformational, not exhausting.

I came to the realization that the journey and not the finish line was the most important component of the race. How you get there matters more than how *fast* you go or even the destination in and of itself. You have a unique purpose. And yes, I know it is sometimes hard to figure out what that is with the busyness of life. But

> **Who is the modern woman? She is tough in the boardroom, nurturing with her family, thoughtful with her friends, all the while taking care of herself physically so as to be healthy and strong.**

it is essential to take the time to discover this in order to live an intentional life.

I knew I had to change how I went through this journey. So I studied and reflected on this for a long time to discern how I should go about this. In this book, I want to share with you the key foundational steps that I have discovered that can enable us to breaking the glass ceiling without breaking ourselves or our families in the process:

- Refocus: Take the time to seek and define your purpose in life at the stage you are currently in.
- Reflect: Be transparent regarding the challenges and acknowledge that you cannot to control everything.
- Redesign: Be forgiving of yourself and focus on relationships.
- Renew: Embrace change, and focus your energy in the right places.

We have the power to redefine who the modern woman is and the path to her success. Throughout this book, my desire is that we can work together to pioneer the transformation and redefinition of the modern woman. My hope is to identify key concepts to navigate us through this process of redefining ourselves and opening up the conversation with each other. It is time to make it okay to talk about how hard it is to be the modern woman and to figure out how to make it better. My desire is to navigate the complexities of life and how to seize the energy to be intentional in leading a life of purpose. I believe that it is possible to break the glass ceiling without breaking yourself or your family in the process.

Let's take this journey together.

# You are Powerful

You are amazing.
You are unique.
You are stunning.
You are valuable.
You are impactful.
You are made for a specific purpose.
You are always enough.
And never too much.
You are a treasure.
You are wonderfully and purposefully made
to impact the world around you.
You are more impactful than you can ever imagine.

You are impactful in every role you have, whether
it is as a spouse, a parent, a boss, or a friend,
Whether life feels impossible or whether you feel alone,
Whether you overthink all the things you "should have"
done or all the things you "wish you could have" done.
Whether you are living to be busy or busy living.
Whether you are focusing on too much.

Or not enough.
No matter where you are in your life,
Your impact surpasses all those things.

You are more impactful than you think you are,
Whether you have it all together each day or feel like a disaster,
Whether you have everything figured out or
just don't know what the future holds,
Whether you are always feeling like life is just
a checklist of things you have to do,
Always exhausting,
Always challenging,
And never enough.

Regardless of who you think you are.
The reality is—you are a transformational
force to those around you.

You are meant to live out your purpose.
And you are strong,
You are capable,
You are remarkable.

Think about those people who came before you
that impacted the world in a powerful way.
Inside of you,
Each and every one of you, is that same powerful person with a
unique passion and strength that is transformational,
With the same impact to this world.

It is now your opportunity
And responsibility
To find that powerful person inside of you.
To find out who you are

And how you can make an impact with
intention in the world around you.

When voices inside of you say, no way, you aren't powerful,
You push that away and take back your life and say
I have a purpose.
I place value on who I impact rather than what I accomplish.
I am an agent of change in myself and those around me.
From here on out, I will concentrate on
the solutions and not the problems.
I will combine my strengths and passions
to propel me into a life of impact.
Because I am Powerful.
And I will live an intentional life.

# REFOCUS

## Pursue and Define Your Purpose

> Develop the ability to completely focus on your purpose so that you can maintain a path of enduring balance.

Keep your eyes on the stars, and
your feet on the ground.
—Theodore Roosevelt

# CHAPTER 1
## Success Is Unique

Have you felt the pressure of a checklist with so many things to accomplish? Do you measure your success by your ability to strike everything off that list? There are so many roles that the modern woman has to play. We have different combinations but nevertheless, we all have many roles. In each role, there is an inherent checklist of things you "should" do.

As a boss, I have to be a great leader every single day (I feel like I can never have a bad day). I must be positive, developing my people, aware of my team, and so forth. The list goes on and on. As a mother, I must make sure my kids are developing physically, mentally, and spiritually—and there are checklists for each of those areas.

I try to do all the things on the checklist, and I still feel empty or not good enough. I came to the realization that no one has it all together. No one. There are many who appear to have it all together, and my natural tendency is to beat myself up and then strive to do it all like that person. But the reality is that one may have success in some areas but not all. This is impossible. Let me repeat this. Realize that success and perfection in all areas of your life is never *ever* possible.

But wait, why is there even a perception that there is only one list and one approach for all the roles in your life? We soon find out that even when we are able to get through the checklist of things, it never feels right or enough. We find out the world's "checklist" was not our checklist and therefore does not always provide us with a successful outcome.

It took me until my late thirties to realize this. There really is something magical about really letting this sink in. No one is perfect, but the reality is, I still believed that people were perfectly navigating through the tangle of responsibility—being the perfect mom or wife or mother or boss—and had it all figured out, put together, and tied up with a nice little bow. When this dispelled myth finally sunk into my brain and deep into my soul, it was a true transformation in the perception of success. This transformation breathed new joy and happiness into my life. The chains of other people's checklists, expectations, and preconceived notions of success were finally broken. But it keeps creeping back in, so it is a constant battle. I figured out that success is unique to me. Our dreams, our desires, our joys are unique to each of us. Why should our definitions of success be measured by the same standards? The answer is, they shouldn't.

Wow! Success should be driven by goals tailored to me! Not what the world defines as success. Each one of us is unique—with different passions, different talents, different goals, different purposes, and different limits. This realization has lifted a weight off my shoulders. I don't take this transformation lightly, and in the beginning, it took some retraining of the mind. After years of comparing myself to others and trying to measure up to them, I still catch myself getting back into that rut of the generic success roadmap versus my own.

★★★

Summertime. When April rolls around, the anxiety of summer bubbles up inside of me. I'm overly anxious to figure out the kids' schedule. I hawk the websites for the various activities and, of course, not everyone has their summer schedule posted yet. With three kids at varying ages, I have to figure out the right balance for everyone. Not too expensive, educational, plenty of activity, safe, family vacation, and so on. Summer is magical for kids but a logistical nightmare for moms.

When I dug deep into what I truly wanted for my kids, I figured out it was not the picture-perfect package of my family. I wanted them to find joy in all they do, to love others (selflessly), be independent, to know how to interact with others, to feel loved, and love God passionately. This was *my* checklist. Society tells me success for my kids means I should sign them up for every lesson and sport, go to the best schools, take my kids to every event and on many vacations, and to be the best at everything. Basically, I should be micromanaging their lives and making them just as busy as I am! Whoa, will that really meet the goals I want for them? Maybe some of them will, but it can also lead to many distractions and ultimately deviate us from our goals. When I tried the generic checklist, I was totally dissatisfied because it did not meet my tailored measures of success and it was just too much.

I know that we all want to lead impactful lives, but how each of us impacts the world will be different. The first step in changing the journey is digging deep to figure out what success looks like for you in each sphere of influence that you hold whether it be as a spouse, mother, friend, boss, employee. Once you define success, you can more easily set goals and limits around it and focus energy intentionally on those goals to reach your version of success.

Sometimes we miss the truth because it isn't what we expect. We have this expectation that life should be a certain way, and if it doesn't go as planned, we become sad and joyless. Sometimes you miss joy because the journey in life is not what you expect. It's about perspective. I thought and dreamed that I would be a stay-at-home mom. For many years I thought it was the answer to my turmoil and guilt for not being able to find balance with my family. I thought that was the only answer, yet in our situation, it was not possible. Even though I loved my job, I became angry that I didn't have the option to stay at home. I thought this change would magically solve all my struggles. Instead, I ignored the fact that I was passionate about my job. Over time I was able to change my perspective to embrace the idea that I could live in the now and set out to find balance and joy with where I was in life.

How many of you know of someone who was impacted by the economic downturn? Do you put your career or your spouse's career on such a high pedestal, that if it gets disruptive, it shatters your joy and your life?

I found myself in this situation several years ago. Life was not what I expected. At first, things were going as planned. My husband had just graduated from architecture school, we were expecting our first child, and we just bought our first house. Then, the economic downturn happened. He lost his job, and we were not prepared for the emotional or financial effect. Most of his friends from architecture school lost their jobs and struggled to find work as well. Their degrees were viewed as "too specialized" and they had to figure out different paths.

No one prepared me for the emotional roller coaster that we went through. It was a dark period in our lives. I felt a burden to carry the family emotionally and financially. My husband was sad and frustrated that his attempts to secure another job were futile. He took odd jobs, and we had many ups and downs, getting our hopes up for jobs and then totally losing the avenue. Finally he took on a very important role of being a stay-at-home dad and then started working at Home Depot after our son turned a year old. It was two years of day-to-day prayer, sadness, frustration, and turmoil. I don't know how else to describe it. Life was not what I expected. It was hard. But when I opened my eyes to those "dark periods," I realized they were blessings. My husband was able to build a huge bond with our son. My husband and I were able to build a stronger relationship with each other and our faith. Our perspective on life changed.

During the storm, we let our circumstances and expectations blind us to joy in the moment and in our journey. When you put the worldly definition of success on a pedestal, you will miss out on joy in your life. If you tailor success to you, if you focus on selfless building of relationships, you will be successful in this life. I didn't think it would be this hard. Don't be blind to an abundant life that is right before your eyes. Don't let stubbornness, how the world speaks, and how you were raised let you miss opportunities to be happy. Pay attention to your transformation in the journey. If you are waiting for the future, you can miss it. You have control of the lens that you use to view your world. The world tells us that we don't have that control but we do.

★★★

Meet Sarah, she was a rising star at the company she worked for. For a decision she made, some people thought she was crazy, but she chose wisely. Sarah was pinpointed by upper leadership as someone who could rise to the top quickly. They quickly progressed her into several different roles, and she got to a director-level role. At that time she had two young children. And to her, she felt like the world was suffocating her. She didn't want to continue climbing the ladder. She wanted to have more time and energy to be with her family. She wrestled for months over the decision to take a step down from her climb up the ladder. Finally, she got up enough courage to go talk to her leader and asked for an opportunity to go part-time. She knew that it could mean a potential squashing of her future career opportunities. But in the end, she followed through with that decision and went on to have another child and was very happy with the balance of having time and energy to give to her most cherished relationships.

How many more Sarahs are there out there but without courage to take that step and make that decision because of fear that they will forfeit future opportunities for their career once their kids grow up, or are just scared of what people might think? Why is it taboo to make such decisions?

Meet Tracy. She has a high-powered job and her husband works full-time as well, but she is the primary breadwinner in the family. She longs to have more time and energy to give to her family, but it's not possible because she brings in most of the family income. Her husband doesn't want to be a stay-at-home dad, and they can't quite make ends meet for him to do that, plus there are not many part-time opportunities out there with a decent schedule. It's a struggle. Even though they have family nearby that help out a lot, they are getting older and so may not be able to help much longer. Tracy and her husband want more kids, yet the daunting cost of daycare and the logistics of juggling the kids' schedules and time and overall energy has shattered that dream.

Yes, I think it's important to have something that you can pour energy into. And it's important to do a good job at whatever you do. But from an energy perspective, we should be throttling it back a little bit and directing that energy toward the relationship side of things. That is a forgotten art.

Consider also the case of Tom and Vanessa, who have two children. Both have very high-profile jobs, work seventy-hour weeks, and don't have family close by. They are exhausted, tired, and overwhelmed. Tom decided that it was best to pursue an even more high-powered job so that his wife could scale back and at least just one of them would suffer instead of both of them. He knew his family probably wouldn't see him much, but at least his wife would not have to work as much. It is so sad that our society forces many to follow this line of reasoning and make decisions like this. Ultimately, this just leads to the further deterioration of the family.

Now consider the situation of Frank. He recently got married, he and his wife had a baby, and shortly thereafter she was pregnant again. They both work full-time. When the next baby came along, he discovered the daunting price tag of daycare, and he wasn't sure how they would make ends meet. The constant stress at work to get to that next promotion was always constantly hanging over his head and causing him angst and stress, both physically and emotionally, with his wife.

Now meet Monica, an entrepreneur. Even though she works from home, she struggles with finding balance to be present with her family. She can't leave work at an office. She can be home but not available to her family. She takes care of the kids during the day and works at night to build her business. With this type of schedule, she puts herself and her own important needs on the back burner.

All these people are doing the best that they can. Nobody told them how hard this was going to be. They feel like they are navigating through this alone. It's not a topic that people feel comfortable talking about. If you were to bring it up in the workplace, you could be viewed as weak even though everybody's going through the same thing. When do we stop putting up a façade all the time?

Do you sometimes feel like it's a game of pretend or make believe? You pretend to be perfect. And if you see a crack of imperfection anywhere, it is stomped upon by people who are imperfect but are pretending to be perfect. How do we change this? How do we foster a culture that is nonjudgmental, that is honest? How do we strike that balance of understanding that we are imperfect but still encourage people to succeed? I believe the key is found in focusing on others and less on focusing on self.

Meet Sasha; she is a director, and she puts so much time and energy into her job and is passionate about it. One evening when she was at home, she saw her thirteen-year-old's diary and picked it up. In it she saw the most heart-wrenching thing: "My mom thinks that we have a good relationship, but all she does is work, and she comes home so frustrated about work that she doesn't have energy or time for me." How would that make you feel? Imagine your children feeling you prioritize your job over them. These are the kinds of feelings that creep into those developmental years and echo through lifetimes.

As we go through this journey together, I want to challenge you to be more intentional with how and where you spend your energy, as well as have the courage to stay on the path to success that is unique to you.

★★★

What do you pour your heart and soul into? Or rather, what do you want to pour your whole heart and soul into? My guess is, it's more of the latter: you don't have the energy to pour into it; you have the desire to, and maybe one day you will when you have more time, when you have more energy, when the kids grow up, when things are less crazy at work. But there is never going to be a perfect time. Listen to that quiet voice, the quiet prompting that's telling you what you should focus on, what your passions are. And take small steps one at a time toward that. Don't try to do it all at once. Just take that first step and second step and third step, and before you know it, you'll be living out your passion with fervor.

Success is unique, and we need to have courage to be different. The first step in building your roadmap to success is defining your key relationships and the impact you want to have in each of them. What are the most important relationships in your life? How do you want to effect those relationships? Remember, success is unique to each of us.

❭ Take a few minutes to list your key relationships and how you want to impact each of them. For example, one of my key relationships are my children and my desire is to prepare them for adulthood.

_____

_____

_____

_____

_____

_____

_____

_____

_____

_____

_____

_____

_____

_____

_____

_____

_____

_____

_____

_____

_____

_____

_____

_____

_____

_____

_____

_____

_____

_____

_____

_____

_____

_____

_____

_____

_____

_____

_____

_____

_____

_____

_____

_____

We either live with intention or exist by default.
—Kristen Armstrong

# CHAPTER 2
## Lead with Intentional Energy

Do you often feel like you are running in place, exhausted but not getting anywhere? Once you have a clear definition of success tailored for you, with goals and limits solidified, you will be ready to run and lead your life with intentional and focused energy that will take you farther and not exhaust you. You will be amazed at how much more you can achieve and how much more satisfaction you will have in your journey with these steps.

Parenting is hard. Marriage is hard. Work is hard. Something that I realized, and come to terms with, is that relationships expose imperfections. Once you are able to accept this, you can then focus on how you can impact those relationships rather than "fix" them (as that is an impossible feat).

Relationships expose imperfections. For example, with kids, as a parent, your job is to prepare them to be sent out into the world. They need to be ready when they are launched into adulthood. So as parents, we need to be intentional about what we focus on to get them ready to be adults. When kids are born, they don't know anything, and as parents we have an important job. Partner with friends and family to help you focus on the main things you want to teach them. But be careful of falling into the trap of trying so hard to teach them every single thing. Make sure you are at least focusing on the main things to prepare them for being launched into this world. You are the shepherd of their future, their guide, but you can use your tribe to help you.

As a working mom of three kids, my days feel short and rushed. Just recently, after a long day at the office, I found myself physically with my family but not fully present. I was sidetracked by the events of the day at work and what was to come the following day. As I was getting my children ready for bed, my six-year-old daughter asked me for something simple—to lie down with her until she falls asleep. I responded that I could lie down for a bit but not too long as I needed to do some work. What she said to me next took my breath away. She turned around, looked up at me with her big brown eyes and said

"Why can't you just be my mom?"

This was a trigger for me to know that I was not being intentional with my time with one of my key purposes in life, my family.

If you think about your life—do you think of it as exhausting or transformational? Why is it that you feel overwhelmed, unable to find the time to pursue your dreams, or be fully present? Have you ever stopped long enough to ask yourself why?

True success is about zooming into those relationships around you. In all the spheres of impact that you hold, whether it be family or work or friends, success entails focusing on the priorities and goals that you need to focus on. Success is being transparent with others and being honest about what your thoughts are. It also is about not judging others.

**Relationships expose imperfections.**

If you want to be an impactful leader, you need to find that inner joy, and in order to find that inner joy, you need to find your focus and put your energy and time into those things. When your passion resonates from you, when you're "in the moment" and focused on your relationships, then you will find joy and success.

We see these new families, with new babies, thrust into a huge additional cost for childcare, the same if not more than their mortgage. They aren't prepared. And these new families, from the very beginning, are set up for failure. It's a catch-22 that one gets into really quickly. Most need a two-parent income these days, but then almost one full income goes to

> **When your passion resonates from you, when you're "in the moment" and focused on your relationships, then you will find joy and success.**

childcare. So then, why do we have a two-parent income? Well, before kids there was a need for both salaries, and now with kids in the mix, there just isn't enough money. This results in pressure to seek for a promotion or job that pays more, which can add a huge amount of stress to couples. That starts the deteriorating of relationships and challenges to a family's mental health and wellness. So what can you do about this?

## Learn to Simplify

"That's been one of my mantras—focus and simplicity," Steve Jobs once said. "Simple can be harder than complex: You have to work hard to get your thinking clean to make it simple. But it's worth it in the end because once you get there, you can move mountains."

I have a tendency to go all out on something that I believe in and am passionate about. I'm not going to lie. There have been many times that I have been overly eager to simplify my life, and I honestly had thoughts of selling our house and getting something small (less to take care of, right?). The reality is, there are plenty of opportunities to simplify our lives. We fill up our schedules with a ridiculous amount of obligations that we become overwhelmed, exhausted, and overly focused on tasks and less focused on the important relationships. I encourage you to look for ways to underwhelm your life.

We have outsourced our lives and so easily fall into the trap of living in isolation. We shuttle ourselves from task to task, but in the end, do we have the energy to foster meaningful relationships? Or do we not have time anymore? Superficiality runs rampant in our society. Why do we allow this to continue? We have a tendency to compare and compete with others, and that typically involves superficial goals of getting more material possessions, status, power, and the desire to demonstrate our lives are "perfect." Is it our human nature of being selfish and competitiveness that drives us? Is it that we want to be the best and attain what the world has defined as best?

If you were really honest about what you wanted in this life and pursued it with fervor, can you imagine how amazing it would be? How many of you have had the thought go through your head of downsizing to something smaller so that you don't have to deal with the stress and strain on your family?

It all comes back to making choices that tie back to what success looks like in your life.

★★★

In the end, are we really giving more, or is it just the appearance of giving more? We are burning ourselves out or burning our relationships out and then we just become broken people, with broken relationships and broken employees. How do we make a change and find a path forward? How do we energize our lives and fuel our lives with passion for everything that we do?

How do we become more present? I'm not just talking about the business books that talk about being present in all your interactions. I'm talking more broadly than that. How can you be fully present and fully engaged in your purpose, in your sphere of impact, in your realm in a way that gives you that life of abundance and your purpose? If you really want to experience true joy and put into effect your true plan, then you have to be fully engaged in fulfilling your purposes. You need to listen to that quiet voice that speaks about what you must do and you must act on what that quiet voice is telling you to do. When you follow that process, you will be fulfilled and find joy. However, this has to be outwardly focused and not selfishly introspective.

How do we transform this messy life into one of focused purpose? It starts with focusing on other people and empowering others to be the best that they can be. I am always on a quest to figure out how to organize my life, my schedule, and my house and how to make things run more smoothly. So I'm constantly looking for tips and tricks to do this. One of the tips I ran across was about organizing one's clothes. It involved a proposal doing this. First, take all your clothes out of the closet and then go through them one by one, analyzing each piece to determine if you wear it much at all. Then, intentionally put back only those pieces that you truly like and will wear.

I did this with my closet, and it was liberating to go through the process. Getting ready in the mornings is so much easier now. I started thinking how we should go through a similar process with our lives. Our lives can become so jammed packed, like a closet full of clothes, with so many things that get in the way that take up space unnecessarily and suffocate the things that are important to you. I think it is important to get everything out, really evaluate each piece, and figure out what is important to you—putting only those things back in.

The other part of simplification is intention with your interactions, and that starts with self-awareness. Self-awareness and self-growth are important, no matter who you are. If you're an extrovert, you have to think about how you impact people and your interactions. Are you talking so much that you're not listening to the quiet voices or picking up on other cues from people because you're so wrapped into what you're talking about? Or, are thinking about what you want to say next and not giving the other person in the room enough attention for you to consume what they're trying to engage you in? If you are an introvert, are you showing passion in your voice, in your body language? The bottom line is that your interactions should be *intentionally* focused on other people—to impact their lives in some way.

We are all human. No matter your level of power and status at work, we all have struggles in different forms and fashions and in different periods of our lives. And it is key that we treat each other with the respect that all humans deserve. Something I learned early on in my career is that you should treat everyone with respect no matter who they are, no matter how they treat you. You may get some easy satisfaction in being hard-nosed and projecting toughness, but in the long run you have damaged a relationship that could require mending at a later time. If

> **Self-awareness and self-growth are important, no matter who you are.**

you take that extra time to be kind and respectful, you can get that respect and support tenfold back later. In my career, it always seems that things come in full circle. Individuals I worked with early on in my career, I worked with again, some of them as my boss and others under my supervision. There is more success and satisfaction in empowering people and finding ways to get people excited about their job rather than just pushing for a spotlight on yourself.

When I was an individual contributor at work with no direct reports, it was so easy to have full control over my work output. I could set stretch goals for myself, work longer hours, find efficiencies, and execute on them. When I started getting more and more people on my team as I progressed in my career to Senior Manager and then to Director, I began to realize that I could not physically do it all. My role then pivoted into more of an influencer. I realized that my job was to drive excitement, set visions, and push for success. My role in the workplace was inverted, instead of concentrated on my own work, 90 percent of my effort went into influencing others. Many of my goals required cross-departmental coordination.

It's vital that you constantly take stock of your priorities and adjust accordingly. Making these adjustments will never be accounted as a failure. You are simply laying a new foundation that will shape your plan of action with a path geared more toward your own version of success.

Take the time to evaluate where you spend your energy and determine if it is in line with your key relationships and the impact you want to have in each of them. This requires a constant self-check. What can you eliminate? How can you simplify?

❱ In the next few minutes, evaluate where or how you spend your energy and time. Does this support your key relationships and the impact you want to have with each of them? For example, I found myself filling our children's schedule with too many activities; the result was that we didn't have much time and energy left to focus on the relationship itself.

_____

_____

_____

_____

_____

_____

_____

_____

_____

_____

_____

_____

_____

_____

_____

_____

_____

_____

_____

_____

I think the currency of leadership is transparency.
You've got to be truthful. I don't think you should be
vulnerable every day, but there are moments where
you've got to share your soul and conscience with people
and show them who you are, and not be afraid of it.
—Howard Schultz

# CHAPTER 3
# Define Your Goals and Limits

M ost people have never sat down to create clearly defined goals that fit with their gifts and talents. Have you?

Tailored goals and limits are the foundation to breaking the glass ceiling without breaking the family. No matter who you are as a modern woman, whether you are a CEO or a full-time mom, your goals and limits will set the path for the success or impact you will have in balancing work and life.

If you are a business woman, you establish visions and goals for your team. Oftentimes, I walk into a new project at work and see the impact of vision and goals that anchor the team to a common goal. This is how you stay focused on the path to success. On the same token, if you are leading your family, you set goals for your family. This fosters community and confidence with your people at home or at work, in your sphere of impact.

Goals and limits you set define the direction that you will take. What are yours? Have you taken a step back from the monotony of routine and examined how directed your path is? Success should be defined and tailored to who you are and what you believe in. The forces that keep the momentum going in the continuum of your success are priorities, focus, and forgiveness.

To have strength and perseverance in this journey, it is essential to ask and accept help from others but also to serve those around you. It is also okay to forgive yourself if you feel you are falling short of your own expectations. You define your own parameters. All of these components weave into the trademarking of your life.

What happens when these components are absent in the life of a modern woman? There are many times that I have found myself in that situation. I was juggling the many aspects of family and work with shuffling kids to practices, trying to manage my workload, trying to be a good friend, and finding the energy to be a wife. I felt like I was always dropping balls and failing. My life teetered unsteadily on the balance beam. I wondered if it was even possible to maintain one's balance perfectly in the midst of the complexities of contemporary life.

> **The forces that keep the momentum going in the continuum of your success are priorities, focus, and forgiveness.**

When I finally took a hard look at my reflection in the mirror, I saw I was tired, sad, hopeless, and hiding my suffering through busyness and a lack of priorities and focused goals—and in the end, trying to do it all by myself. As I finally stopped to reflect on the continuation of this cycle, I became fully aware of the absence of goals and limits in key aspects of my life. At that point, I vowed to be more intentional in my life, to be more forgiving to myself, and find ways to focus on key relationships at home and work.

Throughout our journey in this book, I want to challenge you to trademark your life by being more intentional and more forgiving to yourself. To truly build a success roadmap tailored for your life—not for everyone else.

Know your limits and don't be afraid to ask for help and offer help. Build your team at home and work to fill in the gaps. Realize that you can't do it all, and no one does it all perfectly.

## Intentional Goals and Limits

If you really want to have an impactful life, you must underwhelm your schedule and focus your energy intentionally. Have you ever seen the parent who rushed her kids out the door and said I love you but seemed always to be in a hurry and overwhelmed?

I used to be that mom. I rushed my kids endlessly to all the different activities, from sports, to church activities, play dates, music lessons, and on and on. My kids, my husband, and I were always exhausted. Eventually something had to give. If that's the way you are, stop right now and take a deep breath. It's okay. There are insurmountable pressures to do so many things in order to be successful. You're probably thinking you don't even have time to read a book!

Keep reading anyway. Relax. We've got this.

First, spend some time in self-reflection on what you want to achieve long term with special focus on your key relationships. It's important to think long term and then back track it to where you are now and determine what steps you need to take to get there. For example, when I think about my kids and focus on equipping them to be adults—just having this long-term goal in mind, it puts a sense of urgency into thinking through what it is I want to teach them.

> **Trademark your life by being more intentional and more forgiving to yourself.**

Then I can more easily put together a plan of those key things and set goals throughout the years that are left before they are grown.

Once you have a clear path for each of the success lanes in your life and clarity on what is important to you, I encourage you to display it prominently in your home to remind you of it. Then you can focus on short- and long-term goals. Naturally, you will be able to set limits more easily, because you know what you need to focus on. You don't have to go it alone. We are in this journey together. Making lists are a great way to get clarity in your life. I do this in my own life anytime I feel frustrated or overwhelmed. This is a planning process that really helps you feel more in control.

Once I get through this list, I can then more clearly set up my goals. It's important to do this for each area of your life and remember to maintain a key focus on the relationships you impact.

Are you stuck in some area? It's okay. Together, we'll work through how to fight stagnation and finally grasp that positive momentum forward. But it all starts with taking care of yourself! Follow your own intuition on what you should be focused on now and for the future. It is important to not spend too much energy on who or what is at fault, but rather how you can move forward and progress.

I realized at home and at work, I could create an environment of trust, an environment where people feel excited to help each other, to bring things forward, to build that excitement to get it to where people want to do more, and just create that vision that people want to follow. It's not to say that the times when I had to lead during difficult periods were not tough. They were. It was tough to remain optimistic and maintain energy and a positive attitude. But that was the moment that it was the most import-ant to do those things. When my husband was out of a job and emotionally dealing with it, I had to lead. Many times I didn't do it gracefully or willingly or with strength and positivity, and that's okay, too. Just remember to always endeavor to foster a safe environment and foster confidence in your sphere of impact.

We often don't allow ourselves to take moments to rest, admit frustration, be vulnerable, and be honest with ourselves and others. The ability to be vulnerable and admit you don't have it all together through sharing of your experience is a gift. When you open that door of communication with those you love and those you work with, that's when the magic of real connection can shine through.

❯ As we wrap up this section, take time to refocus. Think about and write down some of the building blocks to help you achieve the impact you want to have on your key relationships. But with that there are limits in time and energy, so remember to prioritize these things with regard to their potential impact and importance.

_____

_____

_____

_____

_____

_____

_____

_____

_____

_____

_____

_____

_____

_____

_____

_____

_____

_____

_____

# REFLECT

## Be Transparent

> Focus on the ability to be transparent
> and admit you don't have it all together
> through sharing of your experiences
> with others. It takes courage to do this,
> but there will be amazing results!

Everything that we see is a shadow cast
by that which we do not see.
—Martin Luther King Jr.

# CHAPTER 4

## Relinquish Control

Leverage the strength of those around you, and don't try to control it all. It's not worth it. Do you try to control every aspect of your life? Here's a confession: I am a control freak. I want things done a certain way at home and at work. When I just had one direct report, it was easier to do. But when I went to a team of twenty, I couldn't control all aspects. I had to learn to be clear on my vision and goals for my team and let them take the journey in their own way. I realized my job was to motivate, inspire, and drive my team to realize their full potential, all the while looking for opportunities to leverage each of their strengths. When I let go of control and led with this vigor, it was amazing to see so many people rise to the occasion and shine in their roles.

In my personal life, I struggle with control. It's not a bad control but a need for knowledge and control so that things don't get too *out of* control. If you're a control freak or just a mom, you may be laughing or identifying with this statement.

For most of my marriage, I thought I had to do the grocery shopping because I thought I knew what needed to be picked out and was "better" at bargain shopping than my husband. So for the first ten years of my marriage I was the primary one to do the grocery shopping. But there is always a first and I remember when this changed. I was nine months pregnant with our second child. Exhausted from being pregnant, chasing around a two-year-old, and keeping up with work, I knew there was so much to do before our baby came—which could be any day. One of those things was to make sure we had the kitchen stocked up with food. My sweet husband always offered to help, and I finally relinquished control of grocery shopping. (Well, of course I didn't relinquish control 100 percent—I put together the grocery list.)

So, on that fine day, I went through my typical process of putting together a grocery list. This time there were about fifteen items listed, and I handed it over to my husband. I was actually relieved to have some time to take a nap while our toddler was napping. As I nestled in for my nap, I got a little annoyed when my husband called from the grocery store. Not only that, it was the start of a very strange conversation.

"Summers, are you sure we need this much stuff?" my husband asked.

Thinking this was a very odd question, I cautiously responded, "Yes, we need all these things to make sure we are stocked up for when the baby comes."

Then, he went on to say he wasn't sure that all of these things would fit into our freezer and refrigerator. Again, it was another unusual comment—especially when I knew we needed that much food and that our fridge could hold it. Once more, I ran through the list of items and didn't see any problem with these items fitting:

1. Ice cream
2. Spaghetti sauce
3. Spinach
4. Milk

5. Bread
6. Sandwich meat from deli
7. Shredded cheese
8. Fruit—bananas, apples, blueberries, strawberries
9. Frozen pancakes
10. Frozen lasagna
11. Frozen chicken and rice dish
12. Ground beef
13. Frozen bag of chicken
14. Frozen enchiladas and rice
15. Bagel Bites

As the conversation progressed, it came out that he had two full grocery carts. This seemed very odd given the grocery list I had provided him with, but it helped make some sense of the comments and questions he was asking. I started asking him why he had that much stuff when I had given him just a simple list.

He replied, "Are you sure we need six gallons of ice cream and eight bags of frozen chicken?"

"Huh?" I thought, and then a light turned on. I have a tendency to go through my grocery list and write, off to the side, an estimate of the cost so that I have an idea if I'm within our budget. So my grocery list looked more like the following:

1. Ice cream 6
2. Spaghetti sauce 3
3. Box of lettuce/spinach 5
4. Milk 4
5. Bread 3
6. Sandwich meat from deli 8
7. Shredded cheese 4
8. Fruit—bananas, apples, blueberries, strawberries 10
9. Frozen pancakes 4
10. Frozen lasagna 8

11.   Frozen chicken and rice dish 8
12.   Ground beef 5
13.   Frozen bag of chicken 8
14.   Frozen enchiladas and rice 8
15.   Bagel bites 7

Oh no! The realization hit me that I didn't put dollar signs next to the numbers, and my husband had mistaken that for the quantity needed. So he thought I meant eight lasagnas, six gallons of ice cream, and so on! At first, he just thought I was really pregnant and overpreparing, so he did not initially question it. But after filling up two full carts, he finally called.

Sometimes it is hard to fully relinquish control. If I had fully relinquished control, we probably would not have found ourselves in that situation. But then I was able to better communicate on my grocery list in the future, and my husband and I could share these types of chores more easily and provide me more energy to focus on more important things. Whether the task at hand is grocery shopping or how to run a board meeting, at times you will need to give up control—make sure you know how to delegate! You know what's important and you can communicate that effectively. Master the art of delegation and watch your family and your team's production skyrocket!

❭ There are things that overwhelm you. Think about and write down what you can get rid of, delegate to someone else, or ask for help on.

_____

_____

_____

_____

_____

_____

_____

_____

_____

_____

_____

_____

_____

_____

_____

_____

_____

_____

_____

_____

_____

_____

Asking for help with shame says:
You have the power over me.
Asking with condescension says:
I have the power over you.
But asking for help with gratitude says:
We have the power to help each other.
—Amanda Palmer

# CHAPTER 5

## Ask for Help

Invest the time and energy into building your village. You will be surprised at how many families try to figure things out on their own without a village, that is, without a community of helpers. Trust me, it is worth the investment. If you are feeling overwhelmed, chances are that other women around you are as well. I know it is hard to find the time and energy to build relationships. And I know it is hard to be transparent that you need help.

Being transparent is hard. Really hard. How can you do that in your day-to-day life? For one it starts with not judging others, and not worrying about what other people think. What you will find when you start being honest is that it will be an eye-opening experience. You will see that others feel the same way and are going through the same things, and the difficulties or challenges that you face will not seem so daunting anymore. That is the power of being vulnerable. It enables others to learn from your experiences. Furthermore, other people may have overcome certain difficulties, and then you will provide them an opportunity to serve you, to help you.

When did we start trying to solve everything on our own? When did we start thinking that it was possible or even attainable?

As you probably already know, by not being vulnerable you live a life that is just going through the motions. It is impossible to fully do it on your own and fully function higher than the baseline. We have become so isolated from our extended family and other people.

I have found that it is so important to have a support group for families, to build relationships with other families going through the same stages in life. This community of people provides a safe environment for support and a wider perspective as we face the challenges of life. Our society tends to leave little time to foster this opportunity. After all, we're all so busy moving from one task to the next, with barely any time to take a deep breath. We are all too busy working and barely making it at home. Nevertheless, I have been able to find this type of supportive community through our church and in our neighborhood.

I know community may be hard to find, but look around at work or in your neighborhood. It can be initiated through a simple gesture of inviting a family over once a month. You will be amazed at how much this will mean to the lives of the family you reached out to and to yours as well. Sometimes this effort can mean a world of difference. What is key though is to have meaningful conversations with them. Be transparent with others and watch as new relationships begin to take shape in your life, meaningful relationships based on a shared and true connection. Be brave in taking the first step in reaching out and being open. Having a group of friends whom you can be open about the events in your life can offer you valuable outside perspectives and a real sense of community strength.

Leverage the strengths of those around you. That is a lesson that I have learned and keep relearning from time to time, especially when I try to do it all by myself. If you leverage the strengths of those around you, the less energy you have to expend and the more energy you save to use toward your family and those special relationships in your life.

When I have most felt like I was "running on empty" was when I tried to do and control everything at work. I ended up working really long hours and only had the dregs of the day left to spend with my family. Trying to maintain the most important relationships in my life and working more and more hours just wore me out. When I realized I was doing this and started focusing my energy on empowering my great team, it was a huge weight lifted off my shoulders. Not only did I

**Leverage the strengths of those around you.**

have more time and energy, but my team had more excitement for their work and more ownership of it. They were empowered to do more and relished the challenge and the trust that I had placed in them. And it was amazing to see the culture of my team change for the better as well to see their development blossom.

At various times my team members had opportunities to go interview for other jobs and yet wanted to stay where they were because we had fostered an environment where people got excited and empowered to transform their work to the next level. Helping people understand the "why" of what they're doing and "how" it fit into the bigger picture drove accountability to where it belonged.

You have to take time for yourself in the workplace, and you have to take time for yourself at home. I had never realized how important it was to take time for yourself at work until I was a director. At the time, I had a large team at work. I also had many cross-functional projects that I was a part of. My time at work was consumed with meetings and fire drills. I found I had no time to just stop and think and process what was going on. It was a merry-go-round of activity, constant movement but always ending up back in the same place. How do you reclaim your momentum and institute changes to make your day fruitful?

I realized that I needed to carve out time a specific time to just stop. I started blocking off time on my calendar and sometimes found places away from my office where I couldn't be interrupted during those moments. The gift of time is the greatest gift you have to give—to yourself and to others. Be mindful of how you are spending it.

## Entitlement "Schmitlment"

Have you ever taken a moment to look around and just see what is happening in our society? It is shocking that we are constantly pursuing more stuff, more activities, and dare I say, more money? The more we seek and acquire, the more we want, and the more tired we become. The more things we get, the more distracted we are from the important goals and priorities we should desire. In pursuit of getting more for our children, we are ultimately failing them because now we are instilling entitlement in them. When life gets hard for them (which it will), they won't be able to handle it. There is no price tag on a relationship with your children. Seek to foster a relationship that goes beyond the materialistic. Shared experiences and memories hold more value than the latest technological gadget ever will.

Yes, you want to reward your children, and they deserve your time, attention, and acknowledgment of their successes but there's a fine line to be observed. The word *deserve* has become a prominent word in our society that does not lead to satisfaction when attained. It is a false hope. Instead we should strive to be a culture of humbleness and selflessness. This is a secret part of joy. Relish in it and encourage your children to relish in it, too. After all, they learn by your example. You don't necessarily need your circumstances to change, but you probably do need your heart and perspective to change. You must find a way to flourish where you are and find ways to maintain laser focus on your goals.. Stay vigilant of your priorities. With this, you can have a life of abundance and joy.

Have you ever wondered, "Why am I happier when I have less?" Look around you. Recognize the sacrifices of others. Instead of feeling entitled, *"I deserve happiness because of this or that ..."* examine outside of yourself. When we think we are owed something and don't get it, we are unhappy. There's a lesser joy to be had if you get something and believe that it is your right, rather than something that is a blessing or a reward for a hard-fought effort. If

> **You don't necessarily need your circumstances to change, but you probably do need your heart and perspective to change.**

something is your right, it doesn't mean you have to exercise it. We are so focused on schedules and money. When we think of what the world "owes" us and don't get it, the result can only be unhappiness.

Take a moment to think back on the times of your life when you were happiest. What were you doing? Chances are the moments you've picked don't have anything to do with material possessions or finances. Why did these times make you happy? Was it just a simpler time, or was it that you were truly present and able to fully enjoy the opportunities that were at your door? When I think about the family vacations, it wasn't where we went that resonates; it was the time together that mattered.

## Constant "Doing"

There are many times where I feel like I am in constant motion from meeting to meeting—answering phone calls and emails, employees stopping by with questions, mulling through the updates and problems, and any other thing you could possibly imagine that wasn't what I wanted to be doing. When I get home, I have children who need help with homework, but I still need to figure out dinner, run them to practice, and finally, push the kids through their bedtime routine. Sometimes, I long for just a few minutes by myself— a place where no one needs anything from me. Do you feel this way?

Don't get me wrong. I love my job. I love the fast-paced, problem-solving aspect, but sometimes things are moving so fast that I just need a moment. I have found it important to find moments—whether it be during lunch or grabbing a few minutes to go for a brisk walk—to recharge and refocus. It is vital to have thinking time to reflect. There is a risk in constantly moving to miss those moments to stop and celebrate success. When there is something great, we may quickly applaud it but then move on to critiquing it and looking for the next big thing.

> **It's important to find moments to recharge and refocus.**

This is where your team at home and at work is most important. Honing into people's strengths, giving people a clear view of their role in the overall picture makes for a much stronger team and puts less on your shoulders. With a strong team on your side, you will have that much needed mental space to recharge and reenergize. Don't be the weak link on the team by taking on so much that there isn't enough of you left over to share in a healthier way.

❭ As we wrap up this section, take time to reflect. Think about and write down the names of people who are in similar stages in their lives with whom you can be transparent concerning the challenges you are facing. Also think about who you can offer help to. What are some areas in your life where you can slow down and be more intentional at home and at work?

_____

_____

_____

_____

_____

_____

_____

_____

_____

_____

_____

_____

_____

_____

_____

_____

_____

_____

_____

_____

_____

_____

_____

_____

_____

_____

_____

_____

_____

_____

_____

_____

_____

_____

_____

_____

_____

_____

_____

_____

_____

_____

_____

_____

_____

Forgiveness is an act of the will, and the will can function regardless of the temperature of the heart.
—Corrie Ten Boom

# CHAPTER 6

## Be Forgiving of Yourself

Have you ever had the realization that some of the things that bring you the most joy may also bring you the most stress? The Christmas season is one of my favorite times of the year but also one of the most stressful times for me. There are so many events I want to plan and participate in and new family traditions I want to create. In my mind, doing all these things is what creates a magical, special experience for my children. I revel in the excitement Christmas time creates through the eyes of my children. The reality is that when we get into December, things start to spiral out of control. All the school parties, church parties, work parties, planning for travel, and meal planning consume every spare moment. Before I know it, there is barely a moment to implement my grand plans, but I still try to cram it in anyway. Not only are we incredibly busy, but I also always forget to include in my planning that we typically get sick during this season. Who has time for that? The reality of what happens during this season is that I am exhausted and filled with guilt—because I can't get to it all—and so often compare myself to others that it obliterates the experience I have dreamed about.

This is the first year I started cutting myself some slack. I set out on a quest to show more grace and forgiveness to not do it all. I still plan marvelous events, but it isn't the end of the world, if for some reason, we don't follow through. Why push everyone to meet a self-imposed obligation if we aren't going to enjoy it in the spirit it was meant to be enjoyed in?

This reminds me of the natural tendency to believe that we are always thinking about the next promotion, the next house, the next whatever, to bring us more happiness. If only we reach the next level, things will be better. Does that really work? I'm sure if you stop and reflect, you will find that it doesn't work that way. When does enough actually become enough if you view achievements as only a stepping stone to your next goal? You may have a moment of joy, but oftentimes the journey to these types of pursuits will bring disruption in other areas of your life— when that goal is reached, it deflates the joy. Instead of enjoying the journey, you may be so focused on the goal that the sense of pride and achievement is diminished; it's so easy to lose perspective. Instead, I have found that seeking joy in what you have and changing the perception of the types of goals that you set is what matters the most. Goals should be focused on others and your journey.

Realize that we are all broken and that no one is perfect. It is so easy to look at other people's lives and be envious of how perfect things appear. It is a mirage. Set realistic goals, and accept that life is imperfect. Remember your goal is to be impactful in your relationships—it is not to do it all nor is it to be perfect in it all.

## Guilt of the Modern Woman

Have you ever felt this way? A tired woman is sitting on the bathroom floor, leaning back against the wall. She is so tired that she can't move. She hears them getting closer, yelling her name. Then hears banging on the door. They keep yelling her name, but not much is registering because she is so tired. She remains quiet, mainly because she doesn't have any energy to engage. The door handle jiggles, and they are conspiring on how to get it open. She holds her breath. To her relief, they run off. She stares into space, thankful for the quiet moment, and lays down on the cold tile floor—so tired. In the distance, she hears arguing and a crash. Then she hears them running through the house, yelling again. She continues to lay quietly—thankful they are distracted and not looking for her at the moment.

Her relief is short-lived. They are back and working more fervently on the door handle. Nevertheless, hearing the persistence of them working on the door wakes her up. It is only a matter of seconds before they come in and envelope her in their realm. Everything turns into slow motion as she savors the last seconds of rest. The door swings open. Three little children emerge in full force, yelling wildly, "Mommy! What are you doing on the floor with the lights off? Come on! Let's go!" and they drag her off the ground. In the next moment, a gush of guilt that overtakes her—guilt that she didn't have the energy to be the perfect parent.

I can relate. Even with our most precious relationships, in moments of utter fatigue, we sometimes feel the need to retreat in order to recharge or reset.

Do you feel guilty about not spending enough time with your spouse, your kids, or your friends? Do you ever feel guilty that you *want* space from those you hold most dear? I have had a lot of guilt and regret in not doing enough in my relationships. I am so hard on myself and feel guilty when I can't do it all. At the end of the day, I realized that oftentimes my expectations were too high and my net cast too wide—to the point that my relationships were being affected. But I also learned that I needed to be more forgiving of myself, to allow myself to not be perfect. No one has it all together. No one. Some provide a perfect presentation of their lives, but it isn't reality. When you are exhausted, fed up, and falling out, I encourage you to get rest and then get up and try again. This is only a season in your life; everything passes, and your dreams are possible in time.

## On the Guilt Trip

Do you ever feel guilty that you aren't available to your kids to attend all their school functions? Do you feel guilty that you come home tired and have no energy to run and play with your kids? That's a working mom's syndrome, and we feel that guilt every day. I long to be home with my kids and to be more available to them, but I also love my job. These two drives can exist simultaneously and often make you feel as if you're being pulled in two opposite directions.

Last night my son wanted to play a card game with my husband. I heard the laughing and the two of them having a wonderful time. Toward the end, things turned sour. My son got very upset because he lost the game. He was sent to his room. Then I heard my husband talking to him, and it really resonated with me. He said, "Son, do you think it really matters about the game? I enjoy spending time with you. I could care less about the game whether I win or lose."

This made me stop and think: Am I that mom who is also a race car driver? Am I "in it" to "win it" or do I know where I'm going and my true direction? Many times I was stuck in a meeting past 5:30, only to realize I needed to jump in the car, pick up the kids, or run to the store. My commute is very focused and stressful as I navigate through the sitting traffic and back roads to get to the day care before they start charging me by the minute. White knuckled and holding tight to the steering wheel, I drive behind slowpokes on the road. Every few seconds, I watch the clock as the numbers climb up to 6 o'clock. Finally, I screech to the parking lot, bolt out of the car door, and race (okay, run) to the front door completely out of breath, put on that smile to greet my children, and start my second job, which is the most important one I have.

How do you find finesse in the midst of chaos? I have been trying to figure that out. The way I feel is the total opposite of finesse—scatterbrained, with too much going through my mind—the schedules at home and at work, what's on my kid's calendar that week, taking care of my aging parents, and staying active in the community. This can overwhelm anyone! Recently as I prepared for a presentation at work, I realized that I didn't have enough time to prepare. In the past that would have really stressed me out. But for the first time, I tried to figure out how I could present myself with finesse with such little preparation time. The secret was to just relax, to be myself, to stop putting so much pressure on everything, to stop climbing toward perfection, and to think on my feet in a real and genuine way.

Be vulnerable. What has happened in our culture where it is more the norm to not be vulnerable? With the rise of social media, we put on the air of how perfect things are, and it's not realistic. When did transparency become unimportant? We ask that of our government but don't want to do it ourselves. Why are we so afraid? We are so wrapped up in what other people think of us that we feel the need to create a false presentation of our lives. In the pursuit of that, we are only hurting ourselves because it is an impossible feat to have a perfect life. Instead, we present this faux perfect life to others and silently suffer. There is one equalizer among all of us humans, and that is that none of us are perfect. All of us have struggles, and we all have successes. We all experience joy and we all experience sorrow. We choose to show only one half of who we really are. Why? After all, we are all only human.

For the first time in years, my family decided to take a whole week of vacation. It seems like a lot of time to take that much off from work. You just don't know how much good for the soul that time did. Focus on family relationships. You don't need to have a fancy vacation—stay in and cook dinner or ride a bikes together. Turn off your phone during family time. All of us—parents and children—are bombarded with information, constantly. Let your eyes be the camera for once. Capture what matters to you in your memories and not on a hard drive.

Do you ever feel like you just can't juggle all the work stresses and kids' schedules and fights with your spouse and all the calendar things on your schedule? I mean the list goes on and on and on and on. Do you feel you have so many good intentions in your mind, things that you want to do, and places that you want to impact, that you always feel like something has to give? That you're failing in some way? How do we create a culture in which it would be acceptable to spend more time with our families, a culture in which there could be, for instance, time off when your babies are born for the husband and the wife to enjoy those precious and unique moments in their family's life?

How do we create more flexible schedules for families to be able to be more engaged in their kids' active lives? How do we create a culture where it's acceptable for one of the parents to take several years off from the workforce and then come back and not have to start from the bottom up again? Some parents have options with nannies and help to keep things running, so that they have spare time they can spend

> **Let your eyes be the camera for once. Capture what matters to you in your memories and not on a hard drive.**

with their family; but for others it's very difficult. Often, their extra time is spent on basic upkeep of their lives.

I know that in my case, many problems began to emerge, some of which had to do with my health and self-care, and it was the relationship with my husband that took a backseat. The most important relationships get pushed to the side. How do our priorities get so out of balance in this one life that we live? Why does our culture emphasize the acquisition of more power and more money over better and stronger relationships? This imbalance is no longer acceptable, not for the future of ourselves and of our children, or of our country. We continue to see the downward spiral, our children seeking attention in ways that are not healthy because they are searching for love and acceptance outside of the home when their families aren't able to provide it.

Think about walking into the kitchen at a restaurant. You see the chefs running around different stations. At first glance, it looks a little chaotic. There are pots and pans everywhere, people chopping up food and putting things on plates, taking things out of oven, and running things out to the customers. But in all that apparent chaos, there is attention to detail and a care that is put into everything, a thoughtfulness put into every step. When the final result comes out, there's a beautiful plate that's fully and purposefully put together with the exact ingredients, perfect placement, and the perfect timing.

The waiter picks up the plate, and takes it from the noisy, chaotic environment of the kitchen, into the quiet and calm restaurant. When the waiter places that plate in front of a customer, the customer is not aware of all of chaos that happened in the preparation; instead when she sees that exquisitely prepared plate in front of her, she feels special and important. I correlate this to where we are in our work and lives. One of the primary objectives in life is to figure out how to see through the noise and chaos. There's so much noise around us that it can distract us from our goal, distract us from what is most important. In the example of the busy kitchen, there are many distractions—distractions that can prevent the chef from reaching his goal. Instead we need to be focused and purposeful in our actions and not be distracted by the busyness of life.

What are some of the ways you can be more purposeful with your time, starting now?

❱ Take some time to think about and write down some
things that you do well and some things you need to
give yourself a break on.

_____

_____

_____

_____

_____

_____

_____

_____

_____

_____

_____

_____

_____

_____

_____

_____

_____

_____

_____

_____

_____

_____

## REDESIGN

# Focus on Others

The ability to understand that you don't have to be perfect and that relationships matter most.

The key is not to prioritize what's on your schedule, but to schedule your priorities.
—Stephen Covey

# CHAPTER 7

# Take Care of Yourself

Do you think it's fair to say that you are your own worst critic? I know I am, and I know I'm not alone in thinking this way about myself.

I've tried all kinds of workout programs that required me to get up at "dark-thirty" in the morning. My typical Monday morning included an alarm going off at 4:45. Immediately, an internal dialogue ensued with, "I worked out on Friday, so if I go tomorrow and the rest of the week, I'll be good," or "I can sleep just a few more minutes and still make it on time," or "I had to wake up with the baby last night, so I'll pass the workout today." Even dragging your feet can be a tough thing to do. On top of that, I wasn't too consistent nor was I eating healthily, so I didn't see much improvement in how I felt.

I hit a period in my life after having my third child when I felt pitiful. I was the heaviest I had ever been. I was tired all the time. I didn't have the energy to smile and show excitement or interest on my face. I felt like it took so much energy just to interact with people. I longed for the moment when my kids would be in bed and my husband would be in his office studying so that I could attempt to recharge my energy and sleep. There were even days when I would drop my kids off at the church nursery and go sit in a corner so I could be by myself. But it never seemed to be enough, and I realized that something had to change. I had neglected taking care of myself, as many of us women do. A transformation of my health was needed. I needed reconciliation with my family, and it started with transformation of myself and taking care of my body. Care for one's self is the first step to being able to care for others in a healthy way.

One of our friends had a wellness and health company. I was at rock bottom, and I asked for help. He put together a six-week plan to go through a healing process based on the food I ate. It was so hard to give up dairy, bread, and sugar, but I focused on the fact that it was just for six weeks. There was an end in sight. It also called for no breakfast—my favorite meal! The first week was tough, to be honest, because I was so hungry. But I kept thinking about the sad state I was in mentally and physically and that it was again only six weeks. Sometimes I made bad choices, but I always came back to good choices. Slowly, it got easier and easier to stay on this new diet, and when I made bad choices, my body felt bad. This made it easier to make consistent good choices. I had to listen to my body and choose to improve my own health.

Before I knew it, I had made it to week 5, and the amazing thing was, I felt great. I had energy. I didn't struggle with wanting to doze on the way home from work. I didn't long for my kids to go to bed so I could sleep. I had the energy to be present. I had the energy to work hard at my job and still have energy left when I got home to focus on my husband and kids. I had better mental clarity. I felt more comfortable in my clothes. As an added benefit, I had lost twenty pounds.

I also found I needed to find time to recharge. I encourage you to give yourself a reboot. Find quiet moments. As a mom of three kids and a leader of a large team at work, I find my days filled with constant questions, problem-solving, and people needing me to be strong, confident, decisive, brave, happy, and the list goes on and on.

What I realized was that taking time to recharge myself was a crucial component of my own well-being. Therefore, I now grab small moments to escape for an hour at the bookstore or coffee shop. I go to lunch by myself and sit in my car and read a book or sometimes just sit and contemplate my goals or pray for my relationships. What are some ways that you can find some pockets of time to recharge and take care of yourself and your life more intentionally?

Taking care of yourself —physically, mentally and spiritually—is extremely important. You can't run the race and enjoy the journey completely without doing this.

At what point did going to the grocery store all by yourself become a luxury event? I know all you moms out there savor the times when you get to escape the constant vying for your attention at home and at work. And the perfect place for that escape happens to be the grocery store. It's a place of pure bliss, where you can walk aimlessly and slowly through the aisles without anyone clamoring for your attention. Our constant rushing and juggling infringes so much on our well-being that going to the grocery store becomes a retreat. You can look through all the options as you stroll down the aisles. Now you can even get a cup of coffee while you shop. There is something about that hour that soothes and calms you. While all the hype for grocery delivery sounds like a great concept, my girlfriends and I agree that it infringes on a precious activity that we hold dear. This just tells me that the modern woman doesn't have enough downtime to think, decompress, and recharge.

Being a mom of three young children and having a career with a lot of responsibility is tough and fabulous at the same time. Amazingly, I can juggle many things and function (barely) on little sleep. Sometimes, it really is a comedy of errors, and I try to just laugh at myself. (Laughter is a balm to many ills!) I have found myself at work with food on my clothes from the morning breakfast with kids.

I was determined to breastfeed each of my children —which meant pumping at work. My goal was to do this for six months.

However, I did not realize the adventures that would emerge from this goal, and I don't know if people realize how difficult this process can be.

Not only is it challenging to find a spot to pump at work, it's hard to find the time to squeeze it into your work day. In my job, I'm in meetings all day. It was tough to make it work, but I learned not to be so hard on myself. I learned to laugh at the situations that I was put in. I needed to relax and forgive myself if I didn't make it to six months exactly. As always, do the best that you can, and plan your next move.

I diligently planned ahead to have my bag with the pump, cleaning supplies, bottles, and so forth. I discovered ahead of time where the nursing room was located several buildings away. When the time came, several hours in, I grabbed my bag energetically and headed to the nursing room, briskly walking along the five- to seven-minute route. When I got there, I saw someone else beat me to it. So I sat and waited a bit, really starting to feel pain. Finally, I got in there, unzipped my bag and started plugging in everything. Then I realized I was missing a key piece—the tubing. My heart dropped. My chest throbbed in pain, and I came to the realization that I had to now drive forty minutes back home to get the tubing and then forty minutes back to to my place of work.

I also had many adventures in trying to pump while traveling for work. There were may trips to hard-to-reach locations which required a lot of travel time. This meant that I had to pump on an airplane or in airports. Not only was the traveling difficult, the locations I was traveling to included construction job sites and mechanical shops. These are awesome places to pump, right, ladies? Have you ever pumped in the tiny airplane bathroom? It is an art to keep your balance and find space to hook into the pump. Not only that, you feel utterly ridiculous, but remember to give yourself room. You are putting forth the effort, but don't expect efficiency or excellence all the time. And remember, it's all right to laugh at yourself or the situation.

> Take some time to think about and write down some key areas that you would like to prioritize in taking care of yourself. Identify some ways that you can fit that into your schedule.

_____

_____

_____

_____

_____

_____

_____

_____

_____

_____

_____

_____

_____

_____

_____

_____

_____

_____

_____

_____

Action expresses priorities.
—Mahatma Ghandi

# CHAPTER 8

## Keep Perspective on Priorities

Not long ago, my husband and I started talking about selling our house. As our family was growing, we weren't satisfied with it anymore. We wanted more room, a bigger yard, something bigger and better. We put our house on the market and within three days we had twenty viewings and five offers. This made us take a step back and conclude that we had a great house. We had lost appreciation for it, and it took others showing interest in it to make us appreciate our home's value and realize, "We don't need to sell!" We also realized that seeking to move was going to distract us from our financial goals.

It was a reminder to appreciate what we had when others liked our house so much. Sometimes it takes something like this for people to appreciate what they have already and to remember their priorities. It's so easy to get distracted by the next big shiny thing.

Women are under enormous pressure to do it all—to be the perfect wife, the best mom, and at the same time, to have a successful career. Every time I have tried to do it all perfectly, I have failed at one or more of them. Over and over in my mind, I have wondered if there could be a better way for the modern women to balance all of these demands. Has the pendulum swung too far in one direction that in our pioneer to equality, we have squeezed out the raising of children? The success of our marriage? We have made much headway concerning the status of women in the workplace, but now more and more marriages are failing. I'm not necessarily correlating these things but merely showing that the more people add to their plate, the more they have to divide their time and energy. You can't do all things all the time. If one attempts to do this, something will get squeezed out.

I realized what I was doing. I have constantly looked around and compared myself to others. So, I was identifying all the great things each woman around me was accomplishing and thinking I was a failure because I couldn't do all those things—instead of realizing that no individual woman was accomplishing all of them.

My children are nine-, six- and two-years-old. Futhermore, I have a big job that I pour myself into because I'm driven. I love challenges, and I love always improving. So, I drive myself. But I drive myself so much that by the time I get home in the evening, I am wiped out. I barely have the energy to make dinner, make sure the kids do their homework, bathe them, clean up the house, take my shower, and oh yeah, spend quality time with my husband. Laughable! It is unrealistic. No wonder our kids are misbehaving in order to gain attention. No wonder our marriages are suffering. No wonder the modern women is stressed and tired and feels utterly defeated. This is a topic that women are scared to talk about too much in the workplace because it shows vulnerability and might hinder their path up the ladder. As I have interviewed many women, it has emerged that this is overwhelmingly the case.

There has to be a better way—a better quality of life. I'm not talking about more money or more stuff. I'm talking about more substance and more satisfaction. We must realize our full potential, uniquely—not how our society has deemed it to be, but what our talents and gifts are deemed to be.

I often find it hard to get together with friends because we are all preoccupied with something—whether it's shuffling kids around, going to work, feeling exhausted, or simply wanting to rest at home. I strive to leave the office as soon as possible, so I can race home, pick up my son from basketball, grab some dinner for the kids, and get him to the gym by six. It's a struggle because some of the kids don't want to go and all are cranky when we leave because they are exhausted from a long day. We rush home and skip baths because we are all worn out by that point. We fall into bed, and before we know it, we are back getting ready for work again the next day. Lather, rinse, repeat ad nauseam.

Our society pushes us to be successful in our career, in our marriage, in our parenting, and in our participation with friends and society. The perception is that if you do a checklist of things, you will be successful. It is a lie. You do all these things, and the ironic thing is, that when you do complete the checklist, you feel empty and so do those around you. From an outsider's point of view, yes, you will look successful but from your own unique insider viewpoint, you have failed. That begs the question, where are you calibrating your success meter, and why isn't it working?

I want my children to have a strong relationship with God, to love others, to be independent, to know how to interact with others, and to feel loved and secure. Society tells me that in order to have successful kids, I should sign them up for sports, lessons, the best schools, play dates, vacation, and on and on. Yet, week after week, my son tells me I don't spend enough time with him.

So, what is the answer? It's really evaluating everything you do to make sure it all ties back in to your overall, both long-term and short-term goals. This applies to your personal life and work life. Being intentional with decisions on how you use your time to make sure it is well worth it—this is key.

When you have clarity about your goals, it is easier to make decisions on how to use your time when life is throwing at you many options that vie for your time each day. Take out a pen and paper. Write out a typical day in your life. At times, mine looks like a fantasy, as the following description of one of my days shows:

It's been a long day at the office. As the time nears five o'clock, I keep checking my watch. I'm already distracted and keep running through my head all the things I need to do (in a perfect sequence) as soon as the clock strikes five. I need to walk quickly to my car. First, I pray there is no traffic. On the way, I call my mom and ask her to get the kids ready. Then, I slide into the house at 5:45, grab the kids, and get to the gym by 6:15. If everything goes to plan, we will make it.

Well, that was a dream! This is what really happens:

At five, I'm ready to sprint out the door, but my boss calls me with a critical work question. I try to wrap it up as quickly as possible and make it to my car at 5:15. Though traffic is spotty, I finally make it home at 6. I rush in and the kids aren't ready because I forgot to call my mom. Plus, the kids haven't eaten dinner. So I'm yelling at my kids to hurry up and get their shoes on. Then, we shuffle into the car, rush through a drive-through for dinner, and I tell the kids to eat fast.

Finally, we make it to the gym at 6:25, only to find there isn't a parking space nearby. We try two different lots and finally find a spot in a parking lot far away. I yell at my kids to hurry out of the car and get everyone to run while I'm carrying the baby. We get to the building, and my five-year-old begs to take the elevator and I say, "No, it takes too long!" Naturally, she is now mad, and I have to demand she take the stairs as I grab her hand. We finally rush into the gym, and of course, we are very late—almost *too* late. I'm exhausted! And the night is just getting started. In the end, planning is not the same as prioritizing.

Planning is making an important list. Prioritizing is seeing what is important when that list doesn't go as planned, and finding joy in these moments.

## How Do We Find the Time to Do It All? We Don't.

My son asked me an interesting question the other night, "What are some of your favorite memories from when you were a child?" As I thought about my answer, it was interesting because all the thoughts that came to mind were about the impact that I had from other people in my life. So I ask you the same question, "What are your fondest memories as a child?"

My memories included the situations where I went out with my parents, who were missionaries, to help people—a visit to some of the poorest areas of Brazil, and people, strangers, who came to our door asking for food, money, and medicine. The most memorable moments where those situations where my family invested in people's lives through the building of relationships and meeting needs, when I saw the joy shining

> **Prioritizing is seeing what is important when that list doesn't go as planned.**

on their faces. That impacted my life. The times that we had as a family when we really focused on each other and not the busyness of life—those moments provided the greatest impact. It wasn't necessarily the places that we went to, or the things that we saw, but the time that we spent together.

To be impactful in this life you don't have to be super genius. All it takes is simply time focused on another person, time taken to understand and be present with that person, to listen, and to be "in the moment." We all can do that.

"Life's most persistent and urgent question is,
'What are you doing for others?'"
—Martin Luther King, Jr.

Don't lose what matters most. What I mean is, don't wait until you are older to realize that you failed to spend precious time with loved ones because you were too focused on gaining more money or material possessions. This possibility scares me. It should scare you, too! That I will wake up one day and realize I have lost what matters most scares me, too. What matters most to me are the relationships that I have. I want to take a step back and look at how I spend my time and my energy. After examining my life, I was shocked at how much of it was not spent on what matters most. What matters most in your life: the time you devote to people or the time you devote to things?

When did we lose transparency? When did it begin to matter so much what other people thought? When did we start trying to hide what we feel from others? When did we start being overly protective of ourselves, refusing to share the struggles that we are walking through? When did we start trying to do everything on our own? We used to have our extended family closer to us, so they could help and support the raising of children and juggling of responsibilities. Families started drifting further and further apart, moving to other parts of the country for jobs, and they lost that nucleus of family that helped provide the needed support. We became so busy that we didn't have time to develop strong friendships and relationships to fill in those gaps. No wonder our marriages have been impacted. No wonder depression has skyrocketed. I think it's time now that we shift to being more transparent and less judgmental of others. We are all people. We are all struggling with the same things. I encourage you to keep that perspective and stay focused on your priorities.

❭ What are some things that you should let go of and give yourself some grace on? Think about the stress in your life. What is causing it? Is it because your priorities are out of balance?

_____

_____

_____

_____

_____

_____

_____

_____

_____

_____

_____

_____

_____

_____

_____

_____

_____

_____

_____

_____

_____

_____

The measure of a life, after all, is not
its duration, but its donation.
—Corrie Ten Boom

# CHAPTER 9
## Relationships Matter

Realize that success is built around relationships and not around achieving more material possessions—that is the secret to finding more meaning and satisfaction. Relationships are the basis for finding joy and purpose in our lives. How do we empower ourselves to build these relationships? Let's walk through this together.

### Serve Others

Do you feel as if you have no more energy to give in order to help others? You really want to do that, but at this phase in your life, maybe you just feel that you cannot do it? I know you think you can't do anything else. Trust me, I felt like this all the time. Childcare for the modern woman is a constant struggle. To whom we entrust our children to is a huge dilemma and one that can be even more challenging when having to do so on a budget. When my friend offered to keep my children, it was a huge help. It brought relief to my mom, relief to me in having to find a babysitter, and relief to our budget.

Serve others and you will not only bring relief to each other, you will nurture friendships in the process. Always offer to help.

## Delight with Connection—
## Take Focus Off Self

My two-year-old had been up every hour, on the hour, the last two nights. It felt like I had a newborn again—except I was out of practice. Then, my alarm goes off at 5:30 a.m. No, I really did not want to get up. Going through my head was the list of things that needed to get done just to get the kids to school and myself to work on time.

Quickly, I scanned my work email from my phone, just to make sure there were not any emergencies I needed to handle. Afterward, I refreshed my memory on my work schedule for the day. Then I try to wake up begrudgingly tired kids. Of course, my two-year-old is whining because she didn't get any sleep either. Then, my husband works on getting the big kids up and going. I am rushing around trying to pack bags, pack lunches, or double-check bags and lunches, and finally making it out the door. In the car, I make three separate stops because each child has to go to a different location and my husband has a farther commute and has to leave earlier. Once the last one is dropped off, I say to myself: "Take a moment. Have a sigh of relief."

But the race keeps going, and I shift my focus onto what I need to tackle at work. On my way, I get a call. It's the first conference call of the day, and I hope to not catch any traffic so I won't be late to my next one—and this is all before 8 o'clock. It's amazing how much we get bombarded throughout the day, right from the very moment we open our eyes. From the moment I come into the office, I have to make decisions and solve problems. In the midst of all that, I need to juggle phone calls, some to the kids' doctors, which entails the logistics of dealing with their new medications.

In these challenges, I have to find those pockets of time to get my work done plus handle logistics for the family. This is how it often goes in the modern life. Sometimes, it's just too much. Imagine this scenario one morning for a mom who is a professional. She had to drive across the street to another building at her work campus. She had to make a quick phone call for work to check in on something as she parked her car. Rushing it and walking as fast as she could to get to another meeting, she hung up the call only to text her husband immediately about something, and then text her dad about taking care of some issue related to the kids. Before she knew it, she had parked her car in the sea of cars in the large parking lot and had no idea where it was when she left for the meeting.

Already exhausted from a sleepless night, she now had to walk this huge parking lot in her high heels and try to find her car. Of course, in the first three rows, she walked up and down, pressing the button to see if she could hear the beep. Then the thought went through her mind to press the emergency button because that would tell her where it is—but that would be too loud. As she was walking, she was hoping that nobody would recognize her and wonder what she was doing. On that day, however, she had on a bright red blazer, so there was no chance of not being noticed. She walked up and down for about ten minutes and then somebody she knew came up to her and asked, "What's going on?"

Finally she admitted that she could not find her car. After going a last round through the whole parking lot, she charged back to the first row that she had started with, and of course, her car was right there, at the very end of that row. She just didn't see it the first go-around. Sitting down, she was so tired, and it was only 11 o'clock. Then, a sea of so much information from people, alerts from meetings and emails and text messages, floods in, leading to exhaustion and frustration. I'm sure you can relate. Most of us have things pulling us in opposite directions every waking hour.

Many times, I'm energized by all this, but then there are times when I don't sleep. Once, I received good advice from one of my mentors at work who said, "Set aside thirty minutes every day. Block it off on your calendar. This is for you. Then, just focus on one thing at a time—catching up on emails, answering emails, figuring out what you need to prepare for the day."

Sometimes we think we don't have time to take that thirty minutes. If you feel that you don't have time for that thirty minutes today, you will probably feel the same tomorrow. It's about making a conscious break from the chaos. Go into the eye of the storm and listen. In there, you will find your quiet voice.

Allow me to give you an example of what it means to listen to that quiet voice. About a year ago, as I was going through the struggles of modern life, a thought occurred to me: "There has got to be a better way." It seems to me that we're all running around like crazy, disoriented people. There are many people who are stripped of joy and have broken relationships. "There has to be a better way," the voice echoed.

> **Go into the eye of the storm and listen. In there, you will find your quiet voice.**

At some point there's another message from my quiet voice inside me that says, "I can't be the only one talking about it." That's where the first small flame of passion began for me about pursuing and bringing to light this challenge. It took a long time to even process the message from that voice. For several months, I just thought about it on my own. Then, an idea came to me, "Well, maybe I should write a book." At first, I thought that was a crazy idea, "I don't have the *time* to write a book! I have no idea how to navigate that."

But over and over, that desire to write a book came to the forefront in my mind. After setting aside some time for myself to think and brainstorm, I started writing things down. Over the Christmas holiday, I had a little bit more time, and we had a road trip to see family. I found time, between family events, to write, using my phone. I even started looking at examples from other books and examined how authors pieced it together and all.

Then, it occurred to me to take a look at a book from an author my husband had met nearly ten years prior. I decided to take another look at his book. I noticed he had a co-writer, and I was curious about this. I looked her up and found out that she had a company called OnFire Books. So I decided just to send her an email to tell her that I was interested in writing a book, curious about how her process worked, and had a passion and a calling for this topic.

Within a few hours, I heard back from a woman named Tammy Kling, and we set up a call the next day. She saw my passion about this topic and the path that I wanted to pursue. She told me that she wanted to help me on that journey and make the path easy for me to go down.

I had secretly dreamed of delivering a TED Talk. At work, I do get up and talk in front of people but it's not always my favorite activity. Yet I did think it was a little odd that I wanted to do that so passionately. As I was talking to Tammy, she then asked me, "Did you ever want to give a talk?" Then, I realized this validated my action to pursue that quiet

**Focusing too much on oneself can increase one's suffering.**

voice. I believe that when you pursue your calling and act upon it, everything will fall into place—especially if it is the Holy Spirit prompting you in that direction.

I have to admit that I was scared of the journey, but when I was obedient and followed those promptings, each step was taken care of—each step solidified and made the calling clearer. And the amazing thing is, the journey was transformational, not exhausting. I don't know the end of the story yet, but I do know that I am meant to be on this journey, due to my specific talents and my specific experiences. Each one of you has your own unique calling, and I truly believe that you will find more joy in pursuing that calling rather than pushing that calling back down by saying, "I'll take care of it later. I'll do it later. I'll find time later for it." When is later? Why settle for later when you can do it now? Have courage to take one step at a time, and it will be transformational.

Let that sink in. When we focus primarily on ourselves, we foster the growth of suffering. When you start comparing to others, you are always going to find reasons to not be happy.

"Try not to get lost in comparing yourself to others.
Discover your gifts and let them shine!"
—Jennie Finch

Why do we choose to walk down these self-flagellating paths of misery when they aren't true to our authentic selves? When we honor our purposes, the light that we generate shines outward, and that is only the beginning of true altruism.

"Your time is limited, so don't waste it living someone
else's life. Don't be trapped by dogma—which is
living with the results of other people's thinking.
Don't let the noise of others' opinions drown out
your own inner voice. And most important, have
the courage to follow your heart and intuition."
—Steve Jobs

### Sometimes I Just Don't Wanna Be an Adult!
Have you ever had a week or two that presented an insurmountable amount of stress? Such extreme levels of stress can be instigated by challenging projects, unrealistic deadlines, difficult employees, or on the home front, sickness of your children, your parents, or yourself, or by any combination of these factors. When life comes crashing down hard on you, it is tough. I know that

when these circumstances occur in my life, there are times that I am paralyzed and just don't want to be an adult at the moment.

It's true, there are no two ways about it. Sometimes being an adult is arduous, but there's a blessing in one's responsibilities in this stage of life. As an adult, you are the master of your path. You get to determine where you focus your energies and how you deal with the choices that are put in your path. Choice and free will come to us with our responsibilities and it is a true mark of adulthood to make the choices that are in the best interest of our own health and well-being, and that of our family's.

❭ As we wrap up this section, think about and write down some areas where you may need to shift your perspective, whether it is realizing you don't have to be perfect, or ensuring that your focus is on what is most important—relationships.

_____

_____

_____

_____

_____

_____

_____

_____

_____

_____

_____

_____

_____

_____

_____

_____

_____

_____

_____

_____

_____

_____

_____

_____

_____

_____

_____

_____

_____

_____

_____

_____

_____

_____

_____

_____

_____

_____

_____

_____

_____

_____

_____

_____

_____

# RENEW
## Embrace Change

> The ability to be aware of what you can improve and rise to the next level.

Every human has four endowments—self-awareness,
conscience, independent will, and creative imagination.
These give us the ultimate human freedom ...
The power to choose, to respond, to change.
—Stephen Covey

# CHAPTER 10

# Find What You Can Improve

Do you know what your gifts are? What do you feel makes you special? Today I want to challenge you to make a one-eighty degree shift in your perspective—to move you from exhausting to transformational and to do that you need to have a firm grasp on three key things:

1. Clarity of your purpose,
2. Clarity of where you spend your energy, and
3. Clarity of your key relationships.

These three things need to be in constant alignment or else you will find yourself right back in the stage of utter exhaustion.

You were designed with specific gifts and a specific purpose. Make use of this fact as you shape your own future and contribute to the lives of those around you. Create a personalized action plan and seek clarity so that you might reach your goals. Reflect on where you are and who you want to be. Take the time to know who you really are and what you want to achieve in life.

A desire to be impactful, to exercise a beneficial influence on others, should be your battle cry, your ambition, and your attitude. Be committed to this and not to any contrary view and you will live an impactful life. The amazing thing is that you have every gift you need to fulfill your calling. And with that, you can live a fruitful life if you are plugged into your purpose.

Ask daily: Into what cause am I pouring my life? Don't spend your life climbing the wrong mountain. Invest in your purpose and invest in people.

Run the race of life with energy and passion, always looking for improvement. Acknowledge that you can do more with others than you can do alone. Figure out how to leverage the skills and gifts of those around you. Don't place value on what you accomplish but who and what you impact. Be radically generous, give your best, and embrace differences between people, which can enrich the lives of all of us.

I spent five years in an internal audit department. One of the main things I learned there was the importance of taking the time to plan. Yes, it feels like it takes longer to get started, but when you do get started, it is focused, well-vetted, and well-executed—you are more likely to reach your goal. It is the same with our lives and relationships. It is important to plan and set goals. Build your roadmap and buckle in for the trip!

1.   *On clarity of your purpose.* You were created to do something on this earth that no one else can do. Take the time to know who you are and what your focus needs to be, in whatever stage of life you are in. Figure out what you have a passion for and ignites your soul.

But I imagine you are thinking you don't know how or have time to figure it out, right? Well, let me share a story with you, that may change your mind. A year ago I had a strong calling to write a book. I had no idea what the next steps would be, but I had a passion for it. I wasn't sure how I was going to accomplish it while working a full-time job and juggling family with three kids. But the key was, I believed in what my calling was without trying to figure it all out before I took the first step. Instead I took one step and then another, and before I knew it, I had finished my book and found how I can impact the world around me through that journey. That

> **If never tested, you will never grow.**

clarity of purpose that I had fueled my energy, and so the journey was amazing and not exhausting. I want to ask you to take the time to cultivate clarity of your purpose and have courage to take one step at a time as you seek to bring it to realization.

2. *For clarity of where you spend your energy.* In whatever role you have, as a boss, an entrepreneur, or as a friend, you have the ability to control where to focus your energy. And it all should tie back to your purpose.

Intentionality versus busyness is another one of the key things that one must do to be *transformational.* What is the difference between these two concepts? Maybe you have a job you don't like but there is something else that sets your soul on fire. Find time after work when you can take steps to pursue it even if it is relatively small and then watch it grow into something important.

Something recently changed my perspective that I want to share. I was sitting across the table from a college student. And I was curious about her perspective growing up in a household where both of her parents worked high-powered jobs. What she shared was very interesting. She responded that her parents were transparent about their challenges and talked openly about them with her. She said that by just addressing the fact that it was hard for her parents to work in those kinds of jobs and be parents at the same time, made it easier, for her, the daughter. And even though her parents didn't attend every event and sign her up for every activity, she had a joyful childhood because they were open, honest, and intentional with each moment. What a relief! This made me think that maybe I don't have to do everything society tells me I need to do to be a successful mom. The key is being intentional with your time and energy so that you can be focused on the moments that matter most.

3. *Finally, find clarity of your key relationships.* The life tailored to serving the special people in your life will lead you to the life you were designed to pursue. It's not money or power but relationships and impact on others that is most important.

## Reduce, Remove, Reinvent, Redefine

Do you feel a constant struggle of busyness suffocating you and distracting you from your focus and purpose? Remember, this life is a journey, and as such it requires constant refocus, awareness, and change. My hope is to show you how to develop a system to reduce the "noise" in your life, to remove non-value items, to reinvent your goals, and to redefine your future path. You may think that you don't have time to develop and you will get to it at a later time. A secret? There is never a better time to pursue your goals than right now! Yet it's critical to stop and reflect. It is important to find time, and I want to provide you some tools.

One method that I use in setting up my goals and limits is to go through what I can reduce, remove, or reinvent in my life.

What does that look like? Let's go through some examples together.

- Reduce—This could be reducing the number of activities in your life. Less can be more.

- Remove—Like the analogy of going through your closet, evaluate where you spend your energy and keep those activities that provide the most impact and remove the rest (or outsource or delegate it).
- Reinvent—Think about those areas in your life that totally zap your energy, but you can't remove them. Maybe it's your job. Think of ways that you can bring your unique skillsets to your job that take it to the next level. Or seek ways to pursue your passion and purpose outside of work even if it is in small increments of time. This will bring you more energy in life.

Ladies, it is time for you to realign the reins of your life. Focus on what is important, and in every area of your life, find what should be reduced, removed, and reinvented. Whether you are a mother, wife, professional—or all three—do your best to add, subtract, and edit your goals in each of your roles.

## Rise

I challenge you to build wealth in all the right places. In order to do this, focus on the relationships in your sphere of impact and the long-range plan that you seek. Live like you are rising, with intentional energy as you progress to the next level in your journey. Always cling to your identity and not to the identifies of those around you, especially not the identities that others try to put on your shoulders. Remember that many women face the same pressures and suffering that you face along this journey. We have been silent about it in the past, but we will not be any more!

I have talked a lot about life outside of work, and the reason is that I have naturally poured my energy into work and have had a successful journey there. Nevertheless, this concentration of my energy on work caused me to sacrifice unintentionally in other areas of my life. That is what prompted me to write on this topic. As I was on the path of breaking the glass ceiling, there arose inadvertently the risk of breaking myself and my family. However, I realize that for others it may be the other way around. They may have family situations that they have to pour themselves or their time and energy into, and this can have a detrimental effect on their careers.

How do we tackle work-life balance? I think it is more of a focus on setting goals and limits, staying focused on priorities, asking for help, helping others, and creating an environment to reflect what will improve balance for you, no matter your situation. With better focus, better care for yourself and others, you can transform your path toward the goal of truly breaking the glass ceiling without breaking yourself or your family.

Simplify and transform your perspective to connect more deeply with others, live more intentionally, and run with more energy in all aspects of your life. Use your super powers to fend off the culture of doing everything on the checklist that society tells us we need to do. Channel your time and energy into breaking these pillars of social expectation. Have you ever stopped to consider that if the pillars are narrow enough they could be construed as bars?

Think about some areas in your life where you are more focused on the frustrations rather than on the solutions. What are some areas in your life in which you want to reduce, remove, and reinvent?

_____

_____

_____

_____

_____

_____

_____

_____

_____

_____

_____

_____

_____

_____

_____

_____

_____

_____

_____

Every great dream begins with a dreamer.
Always remember, you have within you the
strength, the patience, and the passion to
reach for the stars to change the world.
—Harriet Tubman

# CHAPTER 11

## Focus on Your Purpose

This life is short. The focus should not be on selfish gain and building up of material wealth. Instead, focus on giving of yourself and running hard in this life. Know who you are and what you were called to do in each stage of your life. I have learned that to be successful at this, you must humble yourself. We have to be careful not to spend our life seeking selfish gain, with the result that we miss out on the true joy of seeking to fulfill our purpose.

Don't underestimate the importance of the correlation between what is happening in a person's family life and the workplace. There is so much energy put into people's work. As a leader, this realization has led me to value and listen to those who are putting a lot of energy into their work since they are giving up energy from somewhere else. When you lose energy and passion, you get mediocrity. As leaders, we have responsibilities to foster and cultivate greatness. That is when things will compound into more innovation, more passion, and more energy. When ownership excitement permeates the organization, then you will receive a ten-fold dividend. I saw this come to life with one of my employees.

She spent four hours a day, sending out emails at a very transactional level and wasn't very excited about her job. When she was empowered to own the process, she collaborated with other team members to develop a strategy to automate these emails and then spend her time on a higher level, doing strategic work. Now she is excited to come to work and is highly motivated to come up with more and more ideas that improve the company. Maybe another leader or I would have gotten around to automating that process, but if we had, we would have missed out on the compounding momentum that resulted from her owning the change.

As I dig deeper into thinking about my purpose, my focus has been shifting from *doing* a lot of things to *being* what I ought to be and *enhancing* the lives of others. Now, when I talk to my children about the future, it's not so much asking what they want to be when they grow up; rather it's asking *who* they want to be. I want to impart to them that *how* and *what* they do will make an impact.

I don't have it all together. I have a high-level job, three small children, a husband, and a large team at work. My days feel short and rushed. I feel like I'm constantly in the mode of "doing" and I became afraid that one day I would wake up and be seventy to eighty years old only to look back at my life and think, *Was I just "doing" but not living life to its fullest?*

My soul searching began. I wrestled with how to find balance. I wrestled with how to live with purpose. Finally I started to hear and listen to the voice inside me that had been muffled and trampled on for years by all of the "doing." I realized that I had shut out the passion that lives inside me. In my case, it was to write a book, this book. I know every person has a purpose and a calling at different stages of life. If you listen, search, and take the time to reflect, you will hear your calling—and your calling will be about living; it will be about relating to and influencing other people. That is what we humans are designed to do. We weren't designed to be robots—to just "do." We are beings with consciousness, dreams, and the ability to effect change; we are designed for a higher calling.

Great leaders seek to ensure that their teams are successful and taken care of. In your family life, the goal is to ensure the development of your kids in a loving environment and to nuture in them a desire to live in an unselfish way. It's about being aware of those around you and getting messy in people's lives in a way that is beneficial to them. It's about love.

For the modern woman in our culture, the pursuit of a career has become so sterile and too lonely because there is a perception that being transparent of the challenges could hinder career progression. So, we quietly deal with the challenges of juggling home life and working long hours, all the while running ourselves into the ground. This is one area that I would like to open up for discussion in our society; we need to have a conversation about the reality of the modern woman, to break open the arena of substantive part time work, and to create a way for people to live with dignity, rather than simply survive.

At work, I have tried to change myself to fit the mold of those that have been successful above me. However, along the way I have found that it is best to be true to who I am and to build up others. These two things will bring you joy in your career more than the pursuit of promotions. Live in harmony with your true self, not only with your family but also in your work environment. Doing anything else is completely against the very fabric of what makes you *you*.

You will be amazed at the diamonds you will uncover in people around you after building up their strengths, helping them to develop a vision of the future, seeing how they can be a part of the journey, and kindling in them a desire to contribute to those around them. Not only will your team deliver beyond your expectations, you will be more energized and less stressed because your team will be doing more. As a leader, your job is to energize your team, to be their cheerleader, and to be their story-teller. It falls to you to package their successes so that they will continue to work enthusiastically and thus contribute to the overall success of the team.

Inevitably, you will find some workers, who do not step up to the challenge and as a result, they tend to consume a lot of your energy. I struggle with this particular problem. How do you motivate someone who is just skating by, doing the bare minimum? Like a teacher does with a student, show them a measure of success—and see if they reach up.

## Influence

When you are up against challenges, you can choose to complain, be frustrated, take on more work, or you can choose to view it as an opportunity to influence and impact a change. At times, such a change may be placing accountability where it belongs or simply communicating the challenge to someone so that they are aware and can help provide a path forward.

Do you find yourself constantly competing with other women? Do you find yourself examining how well they are doing in their career and family life? I don't have to create a Pinterest wonderland for my child's birthday. Her birthday should be about intentionality not busyness. When you stop competing, you start giving yourself the grace to be less than perfect. You should be focused on reducing the noise in your life that drains your energy and time away from the things that are important in your life. It is important to trademark your life and tailor it to what is important to you and not get distracted by the competition that we women tend to engage in. Focus on encouraging and helping those around you.

The term *breaking*, which is employed in the title of this book, can be viewed either in a positive or negative way. A somewhat negative definition of breaking is to come apart, to shatter or to fragment or splinter. Another, more positive definition is to pull through, to rise above.

In our lives, we usually want to pursue the latter definition: "to break through, to rise above." As a modern woman, at many times I feel that I am breaking apart, in the negative sense. I try to keep up with all the activities and the development of myself and team at work—only to find myself exhausted, guilt ridden (because I didn't accomplish it all while trying to be overly competitive). Then a wake of destruction hits my path of missed quality time in personal relationships. The spiral of thoughts begin: I am broken and have broken relationships in my path.

However, the fog in my brain is starting to lift—partly because I'm on a path toward physical health, but also because I am getting wiser. It is important to refocus and reflect continuously on what is important and to live intentionally in the moment. By being more "in the moment," you will become more aware— not just about what people say but reading between the lines. This is what matters. This is where you can impact true change. Being in the moment is key in leading a more purposeful life.

Does it matter that my kids are signed up and involved in all sports and activities? Or does it matter that I really know the true character of my kids? That I know how and what I need to teach in them to prepare them for the future? Am I driving superficial development paths at work and with family and friends? I realized that I needed to stop just going through the motions. I wanted more and wanted to focus on a legacy that was deep and meaningful and empowering. I wanted to go from good to great. I wanted to be the example to my children and show them by setting a positive example.

The more you do, the more others let you do. That is what I have found at work and at home. For years in my career, I thought I was doing great by taking ownership of things and driving things to completion. I was successful at it, but I was thoroughly exhausted because I took it all on my own shoulders. It wasn't until recently that I realized that at home and at work, I was taking on additional tasks that didn't even belong in my role. Once I found clarity in my role and in the roles of others, it was easier to determine the right ownership of tasks and set boundaries for myself when those tasks that weren't mine crept onto my plate. When I finally figured out how to do this, I was amazed that I could achieve the same results without wearing myself out in the process.

Some key ways to do this are to lay out facts, tell the story, and clearly define roles and responsibilities. I have found that if you put someone's name on a task or ownership of a process or area (even if you aren't sure they are the right person), when that person sees his or her name on the task, process, or area, he/she will quickly speak up and try to figure out who is the right person for the task if it is not him/her. I have found that it is important to frequently go over (as a reminder) at all levels the role of your team, the scope of where your team starts and stops in a process. This ensures alignment with your team and at all levels.

> **Respect your time and give others their own opportunities to shine by letting them rise to the occasion with the trust you are instilling in them.**

I have also found that it is essential to be transparent. Don't try to solve everything on your own. All too often, I see people waste time and money because of lack of clarity in the goal or transparency in communicating a challenge. Have the courage to ask for clarification and timelines.

You can still be helpful without taking on extra work. If someone comes to you with a request that isn't in your area, you can still help by sending them to the right place. They are more apt to complete their tasks as they are more focused. Respect your time and give others their own opportunities to shine by letting them rise to the occasion with the trust you are instilling in them.

❯ What are the areas in your life where you try to do it all? Is there some way or someone you can split the effort with? Is there some way that you can reduce your load by sharing or dividing these responsibilities with others?

_____

_____

_____

_____

_____

_____

_____

_____

_____

_____

_____

_____

_____

_____

_____

_____

_____

_____

_____

_____

_____

There are no great limits to growth because there are no limits of human intelligence, imagination, and wonder.
—Benjamin Franklin

# CHAPTER 12
## Listen to the Quiet Voice

Do you feel there's a spark of passion within you that you haven't allowed to grow into a glowing fire? We all have special talents and desires in our lives. We all have a specific calling and purpose. But who has time to figure it out and much less time to pursue it? We have created so much noise in our lives with busyness at work and at home, that it is very difficult to hear the voice inside you that is leading you to your purpose. How do you drown out the noise to listen to that voice when it is trying to speak up?

### Take It Up a Level

Be the calm in the storm. This is a key component that I have learned to put into practice in the workplace. There is a human tendency to react to challenges in a dramatic fashion, especially in an environment where you have a lot of high-excelling people who are ready to get something done. Such reactions can have quite negative consequences. When such a challenge or road-block happens, I have found that it helps to take a moment to step back and avoid trying to immediately fix the problem. In such a situation, one should take the time to really look at the whole picture to understand why it happened, how big of a deal it is, and if it will bring about an unacceptable amount of change.

There is a truth in the saying that you should "sleep on it." We need to take time to think. Our society is so fast-paced and so "in the moment" that sometimes, we must realize that everything is not an emergency, and that it's okay to take the time to process. It is okay to have a discussion around prioritization. It is okay to ask, "When do you need it by?" High achievers like to get a task done or see a problem resolved that needs to be fixed, but sometimes acting too fast can lead to the wrong outcome. In that kind of situation, we end up wearing ourselves out. Instead, even though I'm not perfect at it, I choose to be the calm in the storm.

How do you zoom into the priorities and goals that you need to focus on? It is being transparent to others and being honest about what where your thoughts are, and it also is about not judging others. That is the key piece for this transparency process—be more open today than you were yesterday. If you want to be an impactful person, you need to find that inner joy, and in order to find that inner joy, you need to find your focus, cache them, and put your energy and time into those things.

Recently, a leader I respect taught me how, in the face of challenges or issues, to focus on moving forward versus honing in on whom or what is at fault. This shift in perspective can make a world of difference in the culture of an organization. Humans have a natural tendency to put a lot of focus on what went wrong and who caused it. While it is important to uncover this, it is more important to rally those around you to achieve a common goal of success for the future. Gaining "buy in" for the future in a positive way will bring a more successful outcome because people will be excited to be a part of it, and they will be more apt to take ownership of it in the future

Let me share a scenario with two outcomes, so you can see the difference:

Scenario: Tessa takes a lot of pride and ownership in ensuring that a technology system is functioning as intended. As she was performing her routine monthly checks on the technology system, she noticed a major issue. She was happy that her monitoring efforts were working, and she immediately reported it to her leadership.

Path 1: Her leadership reacted right away with questions like "Who's fault is this?" and "Why wasn't this fixed earlier?" This left Tessa and the team frustrated because they were closely monitoring the system and took ownership of it. Going forward, it was going to make it uncomfortable reporting things up the chain. It also deflated the team's desire to drive continuous improvement in their area.

Path 2: Her leadership reacted with appreciation for Tessa and the team, elevating the issue. The leaders wanted to understand the process in more detail and asked for the team's thoughts on how to close the gap quickly. They were thankful that there was a process in place to catch such things and encouraged them to keep up the good work. With this response, Tessa and the team were encouraged that what they were doing made a difference, and it made them want to dig deeper into how else they could help improve the monitoring processes even more. For instance, they could initiate real time monitoring instead of doing only monthly checks.

Foster a safe environment and foster confidence in your sphere of impact. If you do this, people will stand with you and relationships will be strengthened or maintained on a higher level.

Look at where you are now. I am professional. I'm a mom. I am driven, and I really wanted to get my master's degree. So I began taking some classes. At the time, I was pregnant with my second child. To be honest, I struggled. When I was in college for my undergraduate degree, I was a straight-A student. But when I was trying to juggle a full-time career, mothering a young child, and pregnancy, I did not do so well in school. (I mean, for the first time in my life I got a B!) I was devastated.

Yet I kept trying harder, staying up later, and finding pockets of time to do my work—but it was nearly impossible. I beat myself up because I was getting B's rather than A's! Then, I had to find a way to give myself grace—grace that it is okay to get a B. I don't have to be perfect in everything. You have to prioritize what's important. Yes, I could spend the time to get an A in school to the detriment of time with my family. But no matter how I looked at it, school fell last on the list of my priorities— ahead of that was family, having my career, and taking care of myself. If I looked at it from that perspective, I was doing pretty good to get a B. Sometimes you need to let go of being perfect.

Remember to prioritize and think about your spheres of impact and the relationships that are important to you or what should be prioritized to the top. Yes, the master's was important to me, to my life, my career development, and my personal development, but I was doing well without it. It was just icing on top of the cake. My family, relationships, my career, and my health—these were my priorities. Instead of beating yourself up for not being perfect in every single thing that you do, remember what areas in relationships are most important, and that's where you should focus most of your energy. The rest is just extra. In those areas, you don't need to try to be perfect. These were my priorities; perhaps yours will be different. It's only important to know what those priorities are and to treat them as such. Don't let what is actually important to you be at the mercy of things that aren't.

Families come in all shapes and sizes. But they all have a common thread. They all are surrounded by key relationships and important relationships. There are times in those relationships that the focus on them is lacking, due to the from distractions of busyness and the complexities of our lives.

It meant so much to me when one of my friends said that she was wrestling with how she could help me with my children after my mother got sick. She wasn't able to help. But the fact that she was struggling with it, trying to think of ways that she could help, meant the world to me. Sometimes it's not just acting, but it's wanting to act and showing that you're wanting to act, that can make a difference. Just that simple thought that she had for me helped. It helped me to realize that I was not alone and that I had friends and people, who supported me on this journey.

## Don't Overthink

I love to think. I crave "thinking time." I believe it is important to think and process things. It helps us to reflect on things, dig deeper into things, and organize our thoughts. But thinking time also opens up the opportunity for you to overthink things—and that can lead to paralysis and the zapping of your energy.

I don't want people to let circumstances and expectations of the world blind them to the joy in the moment and joy in the journey.

We start off our adult lives with gusto and have so much hope and excitement. Then difficulties in life happen, and our expectations aren't met. Our comparisons to others make our lives seem inadequate. We all have the carpet ripped out from under us. We think some people don't have this happening to them, but that's a lie. We all have trials, we all have challenges, and we all struggle. It's so easy to feel down, but you need to find that "pick up" even in the worst of days.

Many of us, at some point, find ourselves having to take care of aging parents and small kids at the same time. I want to share what a typical week could look like when these two spheres of life become a part of your world:

It was a typical Friday afternoon at work. I had my afternoon packed with back-to-back meetings. Around 2:00, I got a text message from my mom saying that she didn't feel well that day, so

I needed to come pick up the kids at her house, as she didn't feel up to bringing them over to my house. As 4:00 rolled around, I had a bad feeling and decided it best to leave early to check on the situation. When I got to my mother's house, I found the kids running wild and my mother lying down in a recliner with four or five blankets piled on her. What scared me the most was she had a gray tinge to her face and she was shaking uncontrollably. Immediately, I told her we were going to the emergency room.

Over the course of the weekend, the doctors identified the problem and were able to come up with and start a recovery plan. I could have lost my mom that weekend, but we were blessed that she is now on a path to a long recovery. Since my mom and dad were the main people to take care of our two-year-old and help so much with our six- and nine-year-olds after school with homework and chores, our lives at this moment completely changed. Both of my parents were at a point where they could no longer care for grandchildren, and now it was pivoting to us taking care of them—all the while figuring out childcare for our kids while at work. Thus, we embarked on sending our kids to daycare and overnight, we went from full support from family to help to none. There are many families that have to navigate on their own with juggling childcare, kids activities, and so on. Extended families are so spread out in this day and age that it has become more common that families have to figure out and navigate on their own so much.

The week after my mom was in the hospital, I found myself in an emotional strain, having to juggle my mom's serious illness, working full-time, and having to figure out a new set of childcare logistics. Of course, that very same week, my two girls got sick with a stomach bug. So, one of those days, I had to stay home with my two girls due to this sickness. It was in the middle of one of my busy weeks at work, and there was no way I could disconnect for the day. I had several conference calls I needed to attend, emails I needed to write, and presentations/strategies I needed to prepare.

That morning, I jumped on a conference call and put it on speaker from my cellphone. Of course, at that moment my two-year-old decided to really seek out my attention. I quickly muted my phone before her constant asking of questions, "Mommy, mommy! Come see! What are you doing?"

I tried to listen into the conference call, in between the distractions with my daughter. The moment she was distracted with her toys, I stepped into an adjacent room. At that point, I was able to unmute the phone and chime into the discussion. Then I hear a funny sound, a loud, squeaky sound. It keeps getting closer and closer and louder and louder. I mute my phone again quickly, and then see my daughter coming up the stairs with a game timer she found in the cabinet. I debate my options. If I take it away from her, she will start crying really loudly. If I try to run to another room and close the door, she may not follow me. But she may bang on the door, so I opted for running to another room.

Grabbing my laptop and phone again, I go to our room downstairs and ask my six-year-old to keep an eye on my two-year-old for just a few minutes while I wrap up this call. I make it just in time to unmute the phone and chime into the conversation again without missing a beat. Then of course, the doorbell rings. I then remembered that my husband scheduled the air conditioner company to come by and work on the unit upstairs. Ah! Just one more thing to juggle in the midst of trying to get some work done. At this point, I'm presenting my screen during the meeting and trying to figure out a way to communicate with the repair man while leading a discussion on the conference call. I muted the call quickly and asked the technician to wait one minute but just pointed upstairs if he wanted to go ahead and take a look at it. I'm finally able to get back to my call and I tried to wrap it up quickly. When it was over, my girls converge and asked for my help. I know you parents out there can relate to this chaos of life!

Sometimes when you are in the middle of difficult times, it is hard to see the joy in what you are going through. In your life, can you think of some difficult times that, down the road, you realized had blessings? It is important to be patient during these times. But more importantly, it is critical to understand and find the nuggets of learning that you can attain from those moments. To influence others, you have to be passionate about what you are wanting the vision to be, whether it is at home or at work. You have to show feeling and excitement and pour energy into your vision to be able to influence other people. What I have found is that communication is the same thing. I know it takes a lot of energy to show passion and excitement, but that is where you will drive impact.

We shouldn't have to choose between work and our family. Sometimes I feel like I have to pour all of my energy into work, and then there is nothing left for my family—especially for my husband. Our society values success in the workplace so much that we lose sight of the importance of our marriages and other significant relationships. Are we putting career success too much on a pedestal?

Are you competitive? Many women are competitive in nature, constantly comparing themselves to others, constantly pushing oneself to perform, to do more in their work, and to perform higher in their parenting. The focus becomes solely on the actions and not on the people. That is where we mess up and start impacting relationships negatively. Competition can be good when it pushes you to grow but not when it adversely effects the energy and time with your significant relationships.

Whatever you're trying to accomplish in your relationships, when you observe others, it should be about looking for ideas—not for comparison. It's taking it a step further and not observing what other people are doing. From there, you consolidate that information and build your own plan for success. Don't reuse another's plans for success. Go through a processing point to consolidate that information and build your own unique plan.

Paying close attention to people and relationships is key to life. Why is it that, with some of our best friends, we can go weeks or even months without talking to them? Of course, we always pick right back up whenever we're back together again, but why is it that we take so much time away from those important relationships? Is it because we become so preoccupied with the busyness of life even at work? As you may note, I struggle with busyness.

There is always a big list of emails to take care of and meetings to go to, and it's so easy to get caught up in all the busyness of work. It's easy to forget about the time that you need to spend with each other and with your employees in order to understand where they are in life as persons. I understand the challenges that you are facing with work. I understand where you want to go in your career and your development. You can't lose sight of the importance of stopping and spending that time with the relationships in your sphere of impact. Whether it's employees that work for you or partners that you work with or other groups or your manager that you work for, or even customers, take the time to check on others and their progress. It is amazing how helpful such focus on relationships can be to your team. It can have a snowball effect.

Have you ever come to the end of your day just looking back and saying, "What happened to my day? How did I spend my time?" I felt like I just ran from one meeting to the next, constantly answering emails and phone calls—only to accomplish nothing by the end of the day. Then you feel completely exhausted, completely drained, and completely stressed about what you *didn't* get done. You may beat yourself up because you didn't do many things that you set out to do, including spending time with your employees and building relationships with business partners. Sometimes we get too focused on the tasks and what we need to get done rather than on the journey that we take in order to get the task done.

Have you ever felt paralyzed by the overwhelmingly vast number of things that you have on your plate at work and at home? Sometimes, are you just paralyzed? Something that I've learned from great leaders around me that, in those situations, one should not immediately react when all of these various things jump at you. Calmly take a step back, and instead of immediately jumping into a "solve mode" or "execution mode," stop, study the situation, and then try to make a level-headed decision that will spring you forward.

Sometimes we hide behind our busyness as an excuse not to pursue our calling and purpose which can be the source of considerable discomfort to us. It is easier to succumb to the busyness and say, "I don't have time to do that. I would love to, but I don't have time." While it is the easy path in the interim, if you do this, in the long-term you will be robbing yourself of true joy, true satisfaction, and true purpose in your life.

The constant pursuit of developing yourself and those around you— is a big responsibility. I need to develop my children, my employees, my relationships, and myself. If I stop and think about it, this task can be overwhelming. Many times I dropped the ball on developing someone at any given time. Sometimes I just over complicate the tasks and expectations that I seek to accomplish. Sometimes I think it's better to simplify what I am trying to do. And we should focus on being genuine and on completing our purpose.

I remember when I became a manager for the first time, and had an employee working for me directly. As I look back to that time, things were simpler. Prior to my manager role, I had more control of my day, and it didn't require a lot of effort from an influence perspective. Now, however, I have close to twenty people on my team. Things are much more complex. There are a lot more people to be involved with, to get to know, and to influence. At the end of the day, there is no way that I can accomplish all the goals by myself. I have to rely on my wonderful team.

Though, it requires a lot of effort to make sure that I am communicating priorities, communicating goals and expectations, gaining alignment, and bringing forth priorities from upper management to roll into it. There is an expectation to be fully engaged all the time, fully communicating all the time, and it's tough enough to hold people accountable for the expectations in my own organization and other organizations as well. There is a constant flow of questions and decisions and analyses that have to be done, along with synthesizing information and prioritizing work. At times it can be overwhelming. At times it can be exciting. That is the price you pay for being a professional, but it is a constant battle to keep the "people" side of things on the forefront, and to make that the most important aspect to focus on. People are the foundation, and sometimes we forget that part and don't take care of our people first.

I remember when my husband had lost his job and could not find another job in his profession for a long period of time. I remember the weight on my shoulders being the sole provider. On top of that, I had taken on the emotional stress that came from that situation. I wrestled with trying to fix it all. One of the hardest things that I had to learn was that *I cannot fix every situation.*

It was hard to find ways to be a supportive wife during that time. Ten years later, I can finally say that I am thankful for that season. It taught us to focus on the right perspective in life—that it wasn't the pursuit of things, status, or money that would restore happiness. It caused us to take a hard look at our use of time and money, and we came to understand the importance of having a strong family, a foundation at home, and a system for raising our children. My husband and I realized that things in this life are temporary, and the true focus should be on loving people, building relationships, and focusing on eternal benefits and rewards. Even though I found that path, it's still easy to get pulled back into the "rat race"of overdoing it.

As I was going on this journey, I met Ruth, who was a college student. She brought to light an important perspective that

I had originally missed. She was about to start her senior year in college, and in our conversation I discovered that was she was a product of a family that was trying to balance all the demands that we have been discussing. While Ruth and her two siblings were growing up, both her parents worked high-powered jobs; even so, she had a very positive view on how their family made it work. Her perspective made me realize that sometimes in the chaos of it all, there are many times that we are getting it right! Ruth is a testament to this and gives hope to those of us in the trenches who are trying do it all.

Ruth shared that her "parents did not have a ton of time for her, but they did have quality of time." Her dad traveled a lot but, he shared his work with his kids and involved them. Many times they went with him on work trips, and these were memorable times in her life that built a strong foundation fo her relationship with her father. Ruth went on to say, "My dad felt guilty that he didn't get to go to all of my games, but I didn't feel bad. I never felt deprived by both working. It made me independent." As I talked to Ruth about what she observed from her parents, she said that her dad sacrificed by traveling a lot so that his family would not have to move and so would have stability. Her mom was good at being present. From a balance perspective, Ruth said that her parents "talked about it instead of just trying to balance on their own. Just addressing that it was hard made it easier." Wow! What an insight! She went on to say that her parents "taught us to reach out for help." All in all, even though I know it wasn't easy, what came through loud and clear to their child was the following key principles that we have been covering:

1. Being vulnerable even though it isn't easy,
2. Focusing on quality time with family, and
3. Asking for help.

## Izabelle—Head of Marketing Latam, Google Cloud

Prior to working at Google, Izabelle was at a company where face time was a priority, and she came to realize that to be a good mother and a good employee, she needed to be in a professional culture that encompassed flexibility. That's when she went to Google. Izabelle said, "It's important to have life outside of work. There are going to be sprints and marathons in each arena of your life—home and work. Each family has to find a way that is right for them. So much comes from *both* you and your spouse; you can't do it alone. My husband loves spending time with our kids and together we are a team. It's not perfect, but we have made it work and it gels well for our family."

Izabelle shared that in our society "there is a lot of pressure. Pressures to be smart, beautiful, and your children to know mandarin by the age of 5." She currently lives in Brazil, where there is more availability of help around the home. But she said that there is risk that because of all the help, people may work longer hours and sacrifice the time with their children. Some things should be outsourced, but we should always make time to be present with our children.

## Mary—Senior Director Technology Company

There are so many struggles for us women. I asked Mary, an incredible career woman and amazing wife and mother, what her biggest challenge was as a woman. She replied: "The biggest challenge is guilt. It is the biggest thing on my mind at any given time. I am lucky; I get to work from home. Throughout this country there are about thirty people who do what I do. I am the only woman. I work from home, and there are very few of these thirty people who work from home."

Mary continued: "Picture the scenario of me working from home: we have a full-time nanny who helps us take care of our kids. Last year I did all of the school events. This year we opted for my husband to be the primary contact and attend all of the kids' events while I worked. It just happened that at the beginning of the year, I had the chance to go to meet the teacher. I didn't have a meeting on my calendar for that time. But part of me wants my husband to go even though he would have a thirty-minute commute either way.

But why? Because I am torn between two statuses. I want to be a great wife and mother. But I also love my career.

If I go, and my boss or a coworker calls and I can't answer, then I feel guilty that I didn't answer it. Because my coworkers who are in this same position have a wife that can do this for them, they don't need to go to meet the teacher.

> **We are still hindered by the stigma that we serve one purpose, one job.**

If I go, I feel guilty for doing something that is outside of work. If I don't go, I feel guilty for making my husband commute, and then I am the mom that has the dad going to stuff. So now, no matter what, I am worried and guilty. There is an endless undercurrent of finding balance between what it means to be a mom and a wife and what it means to be someone who actually wants to be a mom and a wife and someone who wants to advance her career. We are still hindered by the stigma that we serve one purpose, one job."

As we wrap up this section, think about and write down areas you can improve in that will help you stay focused on your purpose in whatever stage you are in. What are some areas that you want to grow in to rise to the next level?

_____

_____

_____

_____

_____

_____

_____

_____

_____

_____

_____

_____

_____

_____

_____

_____

_____

_____

_____

_____

Courage is not simply one of the virtues, but
the form of every virtue at the testing point.
—C. S. Lewis

# Letter to the Reader

Now that you and I have gone on this journey, you now have the opportunity to break open the conversation and be honest about the challenges and odds that are stacked against you. The first step to making a change is admitting the challenge and bringing it out into the open. Speak this out loud and start to take away some of the power this issue holds over you. Let's be honest—our family and our relationships are under attack.

This is only the beginning, the beginning of change, the beginning of talking about the challenges, of not being embarrassed of the challenges and coming together to find solutions for a better path forward. It is the beginning of healing and rising up together to fight for our families first, not money first, not power first but our relationships that are most important to us. That is when we will be successful—when we can truly break the glass ceiling and have a fulfilling job without breaking ourselves or our family in the journey.

We need to change our way of thinking in order to prioritize what is important and redefine what success is in each of our lives. The chains of the old path to success that have been predefined for us are no more. You have the power to redefine your success to what matters most—your family, yourself, your relationships. After having walked through this journey, it is helpful to revisit some key takeaways:

- Refocus: Take time to pursue and define your purpose so as to develop a path to enduring balance. Your success is unique and it is indispensable to have clearly defined goals and limits in your sphere of impact.
- Reflect: Be transparent through sharing of your experiences with others. Don't be afraid to ask for help and be aware of other's needs.
- Redesign: Adjust your perspective whether it is realizing you don't have to be perfect or ensuring that your focus is on what is most important—relationships.
- Renew: Self-awareness of what you can improve will help you stay focused on your purpose in whatever stage you are in and help you grow and rise to the next level.

I encourage you to act. Talk about it with each other. Form support groups with other women, and you will see that you are not alone. Be a part of the change in your life and the lives around you. If we all come together to share and support each other and, ultimately, to provide ideas and ways to make our path, we will make the future better. Help me bring this out of the dark into the light. Become the agents of change in women's lives and in our families' lives. The life tailored to that of service to those special people in your life and your sphere of impact will lead you to the life you were designed to pursue.

This is your moment to change the trajectory of your life. Take back your life. Take back your family. Take back your relationships. Channel your energy to the relationships that matter most. You can achieve a life of success without sacrificing yourself or those around you. How? By living with intention and purpose. When you can find clarity in your purpose, energy, and relationships, you can break the glass ceiling without breaking yourself, and then you can live a life of purpose that is transformational.

An individual has not started living until he can rise above the narrow confines of his individualistic concerns to the broader concerns of all humanity.
—Martin Luther King, Jr.

# Author Bio

Summers Boutwell is an expert at managing the complexities of navigating the corporate world. With twenty years of experience working in Fortune 500 companies, Summers has built her career and family by being intentional and leading a life of purpose. As a professional, a mom and wife, a TEDx speaker and author, Summers knows that life can be overwhelming. She created a life by design that fosters success and changes lives. Summers equips men and women with clarity to implement powerful and intentional strategies to create success and fulfillment at home and in the office. Summers broke through the glass ceiling without sacrificing herself or her family and now teaches others how to reach for their dreams in business and in life with intention and purpose.

For more information go to:
www.BreakingtheGlassCeilingBook.com

or contact Summers at
team@BreakingtheGlassCeilingBook.com

# Notes

_____

_____

_____

_____

_____

_____

_____

_____

_____

_____

_____

_____

_____

_____

_____

_____

_____

_____

_____

_____

_____

_____

_____

_____

_____